January 29, 2020

To Moisha —

Each individual soul
has its own particular way of
understanding the sacred word.
(Barry Holtz)

Enjoy the read!
Enjoy the journey!

Arlene

The Spirits Behind the Law

The Talmudic Scholars

THE SPIRITS BEHIND THE LAW

THE TALMUDIC SCHOLARS

RABBI JONATHAN DUKER

URIM PUBLICATIONS
Jerusalem • New York

The Spirits Behind the Law: The Talmudic Scholars
by Jonathan Duker

Printed at Hemed Press, Israel. First Edition.
ISBN-13: 978-965-7108-97-0
ISBN-10: 965-7108-97-7
Urim Publications
P.O. Box 52287, Jerusalem 91521 Israel

Lambda Publishers Inc.
3709 13th Avenue Brooklyn, New York 11218 U.S.A.
Tel: 718-972-5449 Fax: 718-972-6307, mh@ejudaica.com

www.UrimPublications.com

This book is dedicated to the memory of my grandfather, Melvin Maisel

משה ליב בן אברהם ע״ה

who encouraged his grandchildren to fulfill their potential.

Zaide Melvin played an active role in the building of the State of Israel.
His passion for assisting in its growth was evident to anyone who had the
good fortune of knowing him.

His fourteen grandchildren and great-grandchildren, who live in Israel,
serve as a testament to the values he cherished.

"And Moshe went up from the plains of Moab onto Mount Nebo."

We learn that he saw that in the future that the Land of Israel will be
settled and at peace (Sifri 257).

CONTENTS

Preface   9

Preface

These are the scholars... some rule "impure" while others rule "pure," some rule "prohibited" while others rule "permitted," some forbid while others allow. (Hagigah 3b)

THE SCHOLARS OF THE TALMUD AND MIDRASH, known by the acronym Hazal, had an immeasurable impact on Judaism. Historically, the focal point of Jewish learning has been to decipher the meaning and application of their words. The study of the Talmud (both the Bavli and the Yerushalmi) seems to be at an all-time high. Even Jews who have never opened a volume of Talmud are profoundly affected by its teachings. The lighting of Shabbat and Hanukkah candles, fasting on Yom Kippur, and the prohibition of eating milk and meat together are just a few of the thousands of major practices that make their first appearance in its pages. Certainly it is important to know who these scholars were who made, and continue to make, such a large impact on Jewish life. The goal of this book is to show portraits of several of these scholars according to the descriptions that they themselves set down for us in the aggadic (narrative portions of the Talmud and Midrash) literature.

Some methodological points: I have used several primary sources that span much of aggadic literature, with guidance from the traditional commentators. Though most of these narratives are from the two Talmuds and the Midrash, on one occasion I have used a tradition cited in Rashi that was accepted by the later commentaries. Where there were contradictions between primary sources, the criteria that I used for selection were literary rather than academic. Thus, while the tradition in Tanhuma Lech Lecha

(Chapter 10) mentions a young Eliezer ben Hyrcanus as a refugee from a royal house fleeing a conspiracy, I chose the tradition cited in Avot de-Rabbi Natan 1–2 and Bereshit Rabbah 42 that says that he was a farmer, since it more appropriately fit his personality as expressed in other sources. The same is true regarding the conflicting traditions of whether he started learning as child (Jerusalem Talmud *Megilla* 1:9, *Bereshit Rabbah* 1:11) or as an adult (*Avot de-Rabbi Natan,* Chapter 6).

Since I tried to follow Rambam's advice that translations should not be literal, I have attempted to convey the meaning of the passages to the modern reader. Thus, the phrase *talmidei hachamim* is rendered as "scholars" rather than as the clumsy "disciples of the wise," while the single Shabbat candle becomes two Shabbat candles, the Four Species are shaken (not taken), and Rabbi Eliezer knew the laws of growing cucumbers (not necessarily magic ones).

Although the translations are ultimately my own, occasionally they are based on *Soncino Judaica Classic's Library CD-ROM* (ed. David Kantrowitz, Soncino Press, 1999), *The Book of Legends* (translated by William G. Braude, Shocken Books, 1992), and *Encyclopaedia Judaica* (CD-ROM Edition Version 1.0, Judaica Multimedia (Israel) Ltd., 1997). Dates of the scholars' lives are from *Encyclopaedia Judaica* unless noted otherwise. Any mistakes are mine alone.

This book manages to run the risk of both missing the forest for the trees and the trees for the forest. Readers should be advised that this book does not contain a complete collection of the literature about any given figure. For further research, I would advise reading the relevant sections in *Sefer ha-Aggadah* by Hayyim Nahman Bialik and Y. H. Ravnitzky (Dvir), a classic work that was invaluable in my research. For further reading, one may consult the *Encyclopaedia Judaica,* the *Jewish Enyclopedia* (available online at www.jewishencyclopedia.com), *Ha-encyclopedia le-hakhmei ha-talmud ve-ha-geonim* edited by Mordechai Margolis (Joshua Chachik Publishing House), *Tannaim ve-amoraim* by Yehezkel Cohen (The Jewish Education Department of the

Ministry of Education), and Adin Steinsaltz's *Talmudic Images* (Jason Aronson). On the other hand, the reader should be advised that every piece of aggadah is a world unto itself, so that in the course of my citing hundreds of sources, the poetic beauty and theological depth of each one could not help but be compromised. Those who have the opportunity to sit down and study any single piece at length will certainly be rewarded for their effort.

A philosophical issue that arises is the recent debate in Orthodox circles regarding the humanization of great figures. The debate over how we understand the (apparent?) faults of major Jewish figures ranges from how to discuss the heroes of the Tanach to how we should relate to contemporary figures. Though this is not the place to address the issue with all its nuances, I would like to state the position taken in this work.

Hazal clearly chose to humanize their predecessors and contemporaries in their descriptions, including both the good and the not-so-good. If we ignore what they have taught because we deem it inappropriate, we do them a disservice. They have passed this body of literature down to us so that we could learn from it, and it is not our place to ignore what they have said for pietistic reasons.

I have done my best to remain true to the sources and have noted all the primary sources that are alluded to in the book. I hope that I have remained loyal to the intentions of our scholars and of our traditions. May it be God's will that no error come from my work and that I not stumble in matters of aggadah, and will not say regarding something which is pure that it is impure.

Acknowledgments

I would like to thank the following people who aided in the publication of this book:

My mother Naomi Goldis, for always encouraging me in my writing; my father, Nahum Duker, for providing me with an intellectual environment.

The staff at Urim, in particular Rahel Jaskow, for all of her work editing the manuscript and bringing it up to publication standard, and Tzvi Mauer, who oversaw the publication process from beginning to end. Rabbis Avi Weiss, Hayyim Angel, and Chaim Soloveichik for their invaluable advice. Meir Bienenstock for his creative suggestions.

My siblings, who have been a constant help from my aliyah to the present day: Eli and Rachayl Duker, Josh and Shayna Duker, Yosef and Yocheved Bienenstock, Jay and Sharon Wohlgelernter, and Gershon and Gila Snett. Also Stephen Wohlgelernter and Ezra Duker who we would love to have here on a permanent basis.

My wonderful in-laws, Yossie and Deby Wohlgelernter, for all of their support. Once again, my exceptional mother, whose keen grammatical eye significantly enhanced the readability of this work, and my stepfather, Stanley Goldis, for his advice on technical and editorial matters. A special thank you to my dear Bubbie Selma (Maisel) for all her assistance in making this book a reality. My three boys Noah, Ilan, and Tal, who bring joy to my life every day and fulfill the verse "How good and pleasant it is when all the brothers are living together."

Above all, to my wife Susan. Her support in every possible way facilitated the existence of this book. She helped at every stage of the manuscript, as well as everything else that was required in this undertaking from its inception until its completion. As Rabbi Akiva said, "Who is wealthy? He who has an exemplary wife." In my case this is certainly true.

Finally, Blessed be He who has given life to, sustained, and brought me to this point. May it be His will that I not stumble in a matter of aggadah.

Rabbi Akiva
(15–135 CE)*

Everything is foreseen, yet free will is given. (Pirke Avot 3:19)

No SINGLE SCHOLAR LOOMS as large in the midrashic mind as Rabbi Akiva. He is said to have had the most comprehensive learning since well before the time of Hillel the Elder,[1] and that had he not lived, the Torah would have been forgotten in Israel.[2] Anonymous opinions in the Mishna, Tosefta, Sifra, and the Sifre are "all are taught according to the views of Rabbi Akiva."[3] One of his teachers told him, "You bring concealed truths to light,"[4] and "When a man separates himself from you, he separates himself from life."[5] Both Adam ha-Rishon[6] and Moshe Rabbenu rejoiced in his

---

* The year 135 is given on the assumption that Rabbi Akiva's martyrdom is related to his role in the Bar Kokhba revolt and therefore would have occurred around 135, when the revolt was crushed. There is a tradition (*Sifre* Devarim 357 c. SA II:141) that Rabbi Akiva lived 120 years, which would place his birth at approximately the year 15 CE. If this is the case, then Rabbi Akiva had amassed 12,000 students (having already been learning for thirteen years – see n. 23 below) by the time the Bet ha-Mikdash was destroyed. *Encyclopaedia Judaica*, which does not take this tradition literally, places his birth at approximately the year 50 CE.

[1] JT *Sotah* 9:10 c. SA II:144.

[2] *Sifre Devarim* 48 c. SA II:143.

[3] BT *Sanhedrin* 86a.

[4] *Avot de-Rabbi Natan* 21 c. SA II:154.

[5] BT *Kiddushin* 66b c. SA ibid.

[6] BT *Sanhedrin* 38b c. SA II:139.

teachings (although Moshe had some difficulty understanding them),[7] and God himself defended Rabbi Akiva to the angels, saying: "He is worthy to make use of my glory."[8]

What is it about Rabbi Akiva that caused him to be venerated in a manner that no one else was? His learning certainly played a large role, as he was known for both his methodical categorizations[9] and his endless creativity.[10] But the love of Rabbi Akiva extends beyond his scholarly achievements. It was his outlook on life, which was the driving force behind his incredible life story, that established him as not only a brilliant scholar but as a role model for all Jews.

This greatest of scholars came from a less-than-great background. We are told that he had "no ancestral merit"[11] and was completely uneducated and illiterate. A lowly shepherd scorned by the educated aristocracy, he came to despise those who stood for all that he was not.

> It is taught that Rabbi Akiva said, "When I was an ignoramus I used to say that if there were a scholar in front of me, I would bite him like a donkey."
> His students said, "Master, you mean 'bite him like a dog.'"
> He replied: "No. When a donkey bites, he breaks the bones, unlike a dog, who does not break the bones."[12]

One day, he met the woman who changed his life: Rachel, whose father, Kalba Savua, was one of the wealthiest men in Jerusalem.[13]

---

[7] BT *Menahot* 29b c. SA II:139.

[8] BT *Hagigah* 15b. c. SA II:163.

[9] *Avot de-Rabbi Natan* 18 c. SA II:151.

[10] See n. 7.

[11] BT *Berakhot* 27b c. SA II:75.

[12] BT *Pesahim* 49b c. SA II:148.

Regardless of their different backgrounds, Rachel saw something special in the unassuming, illiterate, forty-year-old shepherd who worked for her father. They fell in love and decided to marry on the condition that he would begin to study Torah. Even with this stipulation, Rachel suspected that her father would not approve of the union, so the couple eloped. Predictably, the secret did not stay a secret for long. Unfortunately predictably as well, her father disowned her and sent the young couple off to fend for themselves. Thus the couple began their married life in a situation of dire poverty.[14]

> Each day, Rabbi Akiva would gather a bundle of twigs. He would sell half of it for food and use half for himself. His neighbors complained, "Akiva, you are choking us with smoke! Sell us the twigs, buy oil with the money, and learn by a lamp."
>
> He replied, "I have many uses for the twigs. To begin with, I study by their light. Then I keep warm with their heat, and finally, I sleep on some of them."[15]

But despite all of the hardship that Akiva and Rachel went through, they held on to their dreams of a brighter future.

> When winter came, they slept in a straw bin. As Rabbi Akiva picked the straw from her hair, he would say: "If I had the means, I would buy you a 'Jerusalem of Gold' [a golden tiara].[16]

---

[13] BT *Gittin* 56a c. SA I:10 #2.

[14] BT *Ketubbot* 62b c. SA II:145.

[15] *Avot de-Rabbi Natan* 6 c. SA II:146.

[16] BT *Nedarim* 50a c. SA ibid.

Two aspects of this period stayed with Akiva for the rest of his life, subsequently influencing his own religious outlook and thus the outlook of all Judaism.

The first is his extreme sensitivity towards the poor. The poor are the "children of the Lord" whom God loves.[17] Rabbi Akiva personally collected money on behalf of the destitute, earning the title "The Hand of the Poor"[18] and teaching the maxim "Charity saves from death."[19]

The other area affected by this period was his insistence on openly expressing love for one's wife, a view that often clashed with that of his colleagues. "Rabbi Akiva taught, "Who is wealthy? He who has an exemplary wife."[20] Rabbi Akiva's affection for his Rachel caused the wives of the other scholars to feel jealous.[21] His statement, "All my learning and all of your learning are due to her,"[22] humbled his students, who felt that they played the primary role in his life.

Although the love that Rabbi Akiva shared with Rachel possessed an intensity that only very few experience, he taught specific *halakhot* that are intended to spark and encourage such feelings.

For example, where earlier scholars had ruled that women should not wear makeup or attractive clothing during the time when they may not have relations with their husbands, Rabbi Akiva changed the law so that wives could be attractive to their husbands at all times[23] (though Rachel herself knew that she did not need to dress up in order to ensure the

---

[17] BT *Bava Batra* 10a.

[18] BT *Kiddushin* 27a.

[19] BT *Shabbat* 156a c. SA IV:3 #269.

[20] BT *Shabbat* 25b.

[21] JT *Shabbat* 6:1 c. SA II:147.

[22] BT *Ketubbot* 63a, BT *Nedarim* 50a c. SA II:145.

[23] BT *Shabbat* 64b.

affection of her own husband[24]). While earlier scholars doubted the holiness of *Shir ha-Shirim,* Rabbi Akiva was able to see in a love song what no one else did: a symbol of the ultimate bond with God. He argued:

> The whole world has never been as worthy as the day that *Shir ha-Shirim* was given to Israel. All of the Holy Writings are holy, but *Shir ha-Shirim* is the Holy of Holies.[25]

The early struggles of Akiva and Rachel, together with their unique relationship, sowed the seeds that enabled these positions to take root in halakha.

At this point we are a long way off from Rabbi Akiva the scholar, since he still did not know an aleph from a bet. How did he rise from complete illiteracy to become such a great scholar? The answer is found in his own attitude. The same optimism that allowed him to promise Rachel a "Jerusalem of Gold" as they shivered in a barn allowed him to promise himself that he would succeed in learning Torah.

Sitting next to his son in first grade as he learned how to read, Akiva began to learn. He never stopped.

> Up to the age of forty, he had never studied a thing. Once, as he stood near the mouth of a well in Lydda, he asked, "Who hollowed out this rock?" and was told, "It was the water that constantly fell upon it."
> Rabbi Akiva asked himself, "Is my head harder than a rock? I will go and learn at least one section of the Torah."
> He went directly to the schoolhouse, where he and his son began reading from a child's tablet. Rabbi Akiva held one

---

[24] See n. 23.

[25] Mishna *Yadayim* 3:5.

side of the tablet and his son held the other. The teacher wrote down aleph and bet for him, and he learned them, then aleph to tav, and he learned them, then the book of Va-Yikra, and he learned it. He went on until he learned the whole Torah. Then he went to Rabbi Eliezer and Rabbi Yehoshua and said, "My masters, teach me the Mishna." When they told him one halakha, he went off to think about it. "This aleph," he wondered, "what was it written for? That bet, what was that written for? This teaching, what was it taught for?" He kept coming back until he forced his teachers into silence.[26]

Akiva learned from anyone who would teach him. At least four scholars – Rabbi Eliezer ben Hyrcanus, Rabbi Yehoshua ben Hananiah, Rabbi Nahum of Gimzo, and Rabbi Tarfon – are counted among his primary teachers. With his diligence and optimism, he soon surpassed them all.

Rabbi Shimon ben Elazar said: I will tell you a parable to illustrate what Rabbi Akiva did. He was like a stonecutter hacking away at mountains. One time he took his pickaxe in his hand, went on top of a mountain, and began to chip small stones from it. Some men came by and asked, "What are you doing?"

"I am going to uproot this mountain and cast it into the Jordan."

"Can you possibly do such a thing?"

"Yes."

---

[26] See n. 16.

He continued hacking until he came to a big boulder. He placed an iron claw under it, pried it loose, uprooted it, and cast it into the Jordan. Then he saw an even bigger boulder, placed an iron claw under it, and cast it into the Jordan. Hence Rabbi Akiva uprooted such big boulders as Rabbi Eliezer and Rabbi Yehoshua.[27]

Rabbi Akiva was able to accomplish these amazing things due to two primary beliefs that he held. First, he believed in the individual's free will, that one can accomplish whatever one sets one's mind to do. With this belief he was able to start learning Torah, assured of his eventual success. "Everything is foreseen," he taught, "yet free will is given." Thus, when Rufina, wife of the despised Roman tyrant Rufus, asked him, "Is repentance possible?" Rabbi Akiva was able to answer with an unqualified "Yes." Rufina then converted and eventually married Rabbi Akiva, presumably after Rachel's death.[28] In Rabbi Akiva's view, anyone can repent, and anyone can become a scholar. It is all in the hands of the individual.

The second central belief that Rabbi Akiva held was, "Whatever God does is for the best."[29] No matter what difficult situation arises, good will result from it. Indeed, after his original period of hardship, Rabbi Akiva seemed to lead a charmed life. Rachel's father, who regretted his estrangement from his daughter even before his son-in-law became an important and well-known scholar,[30] took Rabbi Akiva and Rachel back into the family and bequeathed them with great wealth.[31] Akiva found large sums of money on two separate occasions. God arranged that his debts would be

---

[27] Ibid.

[28] Rashi on *Nedarim* 50b s.v. *u-min ishto,* c. SA II:170.

[29] BT *Berachot* 60b c. SA II:166.

[30] See n. 23.

[31] BT *Nedarim* 50a c. SA II:146, 170

paid, miraculously washing up money onto the doorstep of his debtor. He acquired more money through inheritance and his second marriage.[32] The Divine protection he received can be seen in the following story:

> Once, while on a journey, Rabbi Akiva arrived at a certain city, but was not given a place to stay. He said, "Whatever God does is for the best." So he spent the night in an open field with his donkey, rooster, and lamp. A lion came and ate the donkey, a weasel came and ate the rooster, and a gust of wind came and blew out the lamp. Again he said, "Whatever God does is for the best." That night, troops came and took all the inhabitants of that city into captivity. [Rabbi Akiva, however, was left alone since the troops could not see him.] Rabbi Akiva later said to his students: "Didn't I tell you that whatever God does is for the best?"[33]

But Rabbi Akiva's beliefs did not stem from naïve reliance on his good fortune. He was optimistic before he was successful, and he kept this approach even when confronted with the worst.

> Rabbi Gamliel, Rabbi Elazar ben Azariah, Rabbi Yehoshua and Rabbi Akiva went to Jerusalem together. As they came to Mount Scopus, they saw a fox emerging from where the Holy of Holies had once stood, and they all began to cry except for Rabbi Akiva, who seemed happy.
> They asked him, "Are you really happy?"
> He answered, "Why are you crying?"

---

[32] See n. 29.

[33] See n. 31.

They said to him, "A place of which it was once said, 'Those who enter without permission shall be put to death' is now a fox's lair! Should we not weep?"

He said to them, "That is precisely why I am happy. For now that Uriah's prophecy of the Temple's destruction has been fulfilled, surely Zechariah's prophecy of its rebuilding, that 'Old men and women will once again sit in the streets of Jerusalem… and children at play will fill the streets' will also be fulfilled."

They said to him, "Akiva, you have comforted us! Akiva, you have comforted us!"[34]

For Rabbi Akiva, the only way to look at life is to focus on the positive even in the face of the most terrible catastrophe. This was true for him until his death, which was as legendary as the life that he lived.

It was a time of persecution, and the Roman government had forbidden the study of Torah. Rabbi Akiva's response was to go out to the streets and teach as many people as he possibly could.

Rabbi Akiva said, "I will explain my actions through a parable: A fox was walking on a river bank and, seeing fish swimming hurriedly, asked them, 'From whom are you fleeing?'

"They replied, 'From the nets and the traps that men set for us.'

"The fox said to them, 'So why don't you come join me on dry land?'

"They replied, 'You, who are called the cleverest animal, are really a fool. If we are afraid in a place where we can stay

---

[34] BT *Makkot* 24 a–b c. SA I:10 #33. Dikdukei Sofrim ad loc. implies a larger quote than is found in the Vilna Talmud.

alive, how much more frightened would we be in a place where we are sure to die!'

"So it is with us. If we are afraid when we study Torah, how much more scared should we be when we stop studying it!"[35]

Although Akiva was eventually captured and imprisoned, he continued to teach Torah from inside the prison.[36] He was condemned to be tortured to death, his flesh ripped off by iron combs. Still....

When the time came to recite the *shema*, the executioners were combing his flesh with iron combs while he was lovingly preparing to say the *shema*. His students asked, "Teacher, even now?"

He replied: "All my life I have been troubled by the verse in the *shema* that one should love God 'with all of your soul,' which I interpret as 'even if he takes away your soul.' For I always said, 'When will I have the opportunity to fulfill this commandment?' Now that I have the opportunity, should I not fulfill it?"

He prolonged the *shema*'s final word, *ehad*, until he died as he finished pronouncing it.[37]

Thus Rabbi Akiva went to his death the same way that he had lived his life, with faith and optimism.

This is why it is said, "If not for Rabbi Akiva, the Torah would have been forgotten in Israel." From the time of the first exile until the present,

---

[35] BT *Berachot* 61a, c. SA II:177.

[36] JT *Yevamot* 12:10, c. SA II:175.

[37] See n. 36.

the overwhelming lot of the Jewish people has been one of devastating hardship. Rabbi Akiva's central role in our tradition is one of the things that has enabled us to endure. Although optimism may be suitable when things are going well, it absolutely necessary when we stare at the ruins of the Temple or face martyrdom for our beliefs. We must believe that humans have the capacity for change and that God above is watching with a plan for the best. Rabbi Akiva not only taught this; but also lived it. By emulating his model, the Jewish people continue to move forward, believing that there will be a time when Rabbi Akiva's words will ring true and the prophecies of Zechariah will be fulfilled.

BAR KAPPARA

(Third century CE)*

Rebbi said to Bar Kappara, "Do not make me laugh, and I will give you forty measures of wheat."[1]

BAR KAPPARA WAS FAMOUS for his wisdom and learning. He was not only an authority in halakha, as he is quoted hundreds of times in the two Talmuds and even compiled his own Mishna,[2] but he also was also an expert in Greek ("Let the words of Torah be spoken in the language of Yaphet [Greek]")[3] and the sciences ("Of anyone who can calculate the movements of the solstices and planets but fails to do so is written: 'They do not regard the work of the Lord, nor have they considered the operation of His hands'").[4]

In addition to his learning, he was also a joker known for his stories and poetry. He was so funny that his teacher, Rabbi Yehuda ha-Nasi (known simply as Rebbi), once offered to pay Bar Kappara to stop making him laugh.[5] At a wedding, the guests were so enthralled by his stories that the

---

* Bar Kappara survived Rabbi Yehudah ha-Nasi (see n. 17 below), who is assumed to have died in the early third century. There is no indication of when Bar Kappara was born.

[1] BT *Nedarim* 50b c. SA II:344.

[2] BT *Bava Batra* 154b, *Kohelet Rabbah* 6:2.

[3] *Bereshit Rabbah* 36:8.

[4] BT *Shabbat* 75a

[5] See note 1.

food went untouched.[6] But one day he took the joke too far, starting a feud between him and his beloved teacher.

Bar Kappara looked up to Rebbi, studied his teachings, and asked for his advice on personal matters.[7] Devoted to Rebbi's teachings, he went so far as to swear his faithfulness in transmitting them.[8] Nevertheless, he felt slighted by his teacher, and it is easy to see why. A short glimpse into Rebbi's world reveals the source of Bar Kappara's unhappiness.

Rebbi was not only one of the most important scholars – it is his version of the Mishna which became part of the canon – but he was also an aristocrat, born into a wealthy and powerful family who shared the values of that lifestyle. Rebbi held the title of Nasi, the political head of Israel's Jewish community who was recognized by the Roman government, a position that he inherited because of his pedigree. Along with his position he inherited great wealth. He had guards (possibly eunuchs!) who protected him, exacting revenge on anyone who tried to do him harm.[9] And like much of the aristocracy, he valued wealth and those who possessed it. As the Talmud bluntly puts it, "Rebbi showed respect to rich men." He would openly announce the wealth that his guests possessed and insult rich men who did not dress the part.[10] For his son-in-law he chose Ben Elash, a man who had much more money than wisdom, whose hairstyle was handsome but whose mind was not sharp enough for the discussions between Rebbi and Bar Kappara.[11]

No matter how much he studied, Bar Kappara could not win his master's affection in this area. There is no mention of his wealth, and his

---

6 *Va-Yikra Rabbah* 28:2, *Kohelet Rabbah* 1:4 c. SA II:340.

7 BT *Berakhot* 56b c. SA II:346.

8 BT *Yevamot* 32b.

9 BT *Berakhot* 16b, Rashi ad loc. s.v. *"ve-af,"* Soncino Talmud ad loc. n 22.

10 BT *Eruvin* 85a c. SA II:316.

11 BT *Nedarim* 51a, BT *Sanhedrin* 22b.

intensity in collecting wheat clearly displays his need for it.[12] Any respect that the Roman government gave to him came from his good deeds rather from his wealth and pedigree.[13] He could not help but feel disdain for those who won Rebbi's respect by possessing what he would never have.

But, as mentioned before, Bar Kappara had a sense of humor. So he decided to play a joke on Ben Elash, Rebbi's ignorant but wealthy son-in-law. He told Ben Elash, "Everyone asks Rebbi halakhic questions except for you," subtly suggesting that Bar Elash should ask one of his own. Not knowing what to ask, Bar Elash asked Bar Kappara for advice. Bar Kappara suggested that he recite a riddle for Rebbi. And when he did, Rebbi was furious.

What was this riddle? It started with a play on the name Elash, which shares the same letters as the Hebrew world for "lowest place," and continues with jabs at Rebbi's authority.

> He who is lowest of the low manages to look down from heaven.
> Inside whom is he operating?
> From whom terrified scholars' minds take wing, young scholars see him and hide, and old men stand up in deference.
> He who avoids him is happy,
> But one who gets stuck honoring him is trapped.

Upon hearing the naïve Ben Elash recite this in total sincerity, Rebbi turned around to see Bar Kappara chuckling. Rebbi immediately understood what had happened. Looking directly at Bar Kappara, he said, "Elder, I don't

---

[12] See note 1.

[13] *Kohelet Rabbah* 11:1 #1 c. SA II:346.

think I know who you are." We are told that then and there Bar Kappara was certain that he would not be ordained.[14]

From that point, things began to deteriorate further. While learning with Rebbi's son Shimon, Bar Kappara insulted his former teacher. Predictably, Shimon told his father, and Bar Kappara was placed under a thirty-day ban.[15]

Then, when Shimon was getting married, Rebbi did not invite Bar Kappara to the wedding. Attempting to comfort himself, Bar Kappara said, "If those who do not do His will are so well off, how much better off will be those who do His will?" Nevertheless, Bar Kappara was hurt and upset, and the action he took was a bit extreme. First, he wrote on the door to the dining hall, "All rejoicing ends in death, so of what value is your rejoicing?" Rebbi did not have to look far to see who the culprit was, for on the pavilion under the *huppah* it was written, "Twenty-four thousand myriads of dinars [currency] were spent for the pavilion, yet the father of the groom did not invite Bar Kappara."

However, even as Bar Kappara's sharp tongue got him into trouble, it was the same tongue that put him back into Rebbi's good graces. Hearing Bar Kappara's new slogan – "If those who do not do His will are so well off, how much better off will be those who do his will" – gave him a clue as to what was wrong. Mindful now of the gap between those who are well off and those who are not, Rebbi reconsidered and invited Bar Kappara. "They apologized to each other and made peace."[16] With that, teacher and student were reunited, and Bar Kappara once again became a faithful transmitter of Rebbi's traditions.

In the end, when Rebbi passed from this world, it was Bar Kappara's poetry that delivered the most touching eulogy:

---

[14] JT *Moed Katan* 3:1 c. SA II: 342.

[15] BT *Moed Katan* 16b c. SA II:343.

[16] BT *Nedarim* 50b, *Va-Yikra Rabbah* 28:2, *Kohelet Rabbah* 1:4 c. SA II: 340–341

Angels and mortals have been wrestling for the Holy Ark;
The angels have won and the Holy Ark has been taken.[17]

---

[17] BT *Ketubbot* 104a, *Kohelet Rabbah* 7:19 c. SA II:328.

RABBI ELAZAR BEN RABBI SHIMON

(Second–third century CE)

Rabbi Shimon bar Yochai used to say: I see those that will see the Divine Presence in the next world, and they are few. If there are a thousand, I and my son are among them. If there are one hundred, I and my son are among them. If there are only two, I and my son are the ones.[1]

A YOUNG MAN, the son of a great scholar, showed no interest in studying Torah. A great rabbi, confident that the son would follow in his father's footsteps if only he had the right training, took him under his wing. Thus began the scholarly life of Elazar, the son of Rabbi Shimon bar Yochai.[2]

As Rabbi Elazar grew up, he had no interest in learning Torah. Although his father, Rabbi Shimon, was one of Rabbi Akiva's greatest students, Elazar was interested in more physical pursuits. A strong, burly boy, he liked to show off. Once, when some donkey drivers teased him about his unusual eating habits (he would sit near the oven while his mother constantly baked bread, eating until there was no more dough in the house), he retaliated against the perceived slight by carrying all of their donkeys up to the roof of his house. Upon his father's orders he took them down, but not without showing off a little more – while he had carried them up one by one, he took them down two at a time.[3] The local scholars knew that Elazar

---

[1] BT *Sukkah* 45b c. SA II:218.

[2] *Tanhuma* (ed. Buber), Va-Yera 38c. SA II:230.

[3] *Pesikta de-Rav Kahana* (ed. Mandelbaum) 11:18 c. SA II:229.

had no interest in studying Torah and that he spent his days working as a porter.

One day, an old man asked him to load up a donkey for him and his baggage. Elazar laughed. "Look at this old man," he told the bystanders. "I could load him on my back and carry him myself to the end of the world." And, true to his word, he put the man on his back and began to carry him to his destination.

A physically impressive build might not be a characteristic of a future Torah scholar. But some people who saw through Elazar's façade urged him to realize his potential. One of them was the old man, who was really Eliyahu ha-Navi in disguise.[4]

Another person who saw Elazar's potential was Rabbi Yose ben Halafta. Much to the chagrin of his colleagues, especially Rabbi Yehuda, he took Elazar under his wing and began to teach him Torah. A few years later Elazar was answering questions put to him by the greatest scholars, until even the skeptical Rabbi Yehuda was won over.[5]

It was an enormous change for Elazar. All the strength and intensity he had once devoted to physical accomplishments he now turned to his studies. While before he could carry donkeys up and down stairs, once he began to study Torah, "he could not even carry his own cloak."[6] As if his youthful, single-minded dedication were not enough, events occurred that intensified it even more.

Elazar's father, Rabbi Shimon bar Yochai, was quite an intense man himself. As a child, he was dissatisfied with his mother's level of observance. "Whenever he saw his mother engaging in long chats on Shabbat, he would say, 'Mother, it's Shabbat!'"[7] Rabbi Shimon had nothing but scorn for his

---

[4] *Pesikta de-Rav Kahan* 11:22 c. SA II:231.

[5] See n. 2.

[6] See n. 3.

[7] JT *Shabbat* 15:3 c. SA II:227.

father, an informer for the Roman government, and grew to reject everything that his father represented.[8] His hatred for the Romans only intensified as he saw his teachers and colleagues hunted down and killed, until the only teachers of Torah left were himself and four other students of Rabbi Akiva.[9] His famous saying, "It is a known fact that Esav (Rome) hates Yaakov (Jews),"[10] is an accurate portrayal of his world view. His anti-Roman sentiment probably led him to be watched as a potential rebel, and it was only a matter of time before the Romans found an excuse to persecute him.

> On one occasion while Rabbi Yehuda, Rabbi Yose, and Rabbi Shimon were sitting together, Yehuda the Son of Converts was sitting with them. Rabbi Yehuda began the discussion by saying, "How great are the works of the Roman government! They laid out streets, erected bridges, and built baths." Rabbi Yose remained silent, but Rabbi Shimon spoke up and said, "All that they did was only to serve themselves. They laid out streets to put prostitutes on them, built baths to pamper themselves, and erected bridges to levy tolls." Yehuda the Son of Converts then went off and kept retelling what had happened until the Roman government heard about it. The Romans decreed that "Yehuda who spoke well shall be promoted, Yose who remained silent shall be exiled, and Shimon who criticized shall be killed."[11]

---

[8] BT *Pesahim* 112a.

[9] BT *Yevamot* 62b. *Bereshit Rabbah* 61:3 lists six other students.

[10] *Sifri Ba-midbar* 69.

[11] BT *Shabbat* 33b c. SA II:221.

Somehow, Elazar found himself caught up in his father's alleged act of treason. Perhaps he made similar statements himself, was suspected because of his father, or simply wanted to keep his fugitive father company. Whatever the reason, Elazar went on the run with his father. At first they hid out in the academy and Elazar's mother delivered food to them. Then, fearing that she would be tortured for information on their location, they ran away to a cave as to keep their whereabouts secret.

> God created a carob tree and a well for them. Taking off their clothes in order to keep them from wearing out, the father and son sat buried in sand up to their necks, studying the entire day. When it was time to pray, they would put on their clothes, wrap themselves in their prayer shawls, and pray. Then they would take off their clothes again and cover themselves with sand. They stayed in the cave for twelve years.[12]

The effect of this time on Elazar was enormous. He was already intensely devoted to Torah, and this experience removed him entirely from the outside world. Cut off from everyday life, with food miraculously provided for him, all that concerned him now were study and prayer. He began to see this way of life as ideal and therefore saw himself and his father as ideal people. As Rabbi Shimon said, "I have seen those who will see the Divine Presence in the next world, and they are few.... If there are only two people, I and my son are the ones."[13] Learning Torah was not only important; it was the only thing of importance. Anyone who did not realize that was wasting his life and was therefore not worthy of it. Thus, when the emperor died and they were finally able to leave the cave, the shock of the outside world hit them all the harder.

---

[12] Ibid.

[13] See note 1 above.

When they went outside, they saw people plowing and sowing. R Shimon exclaimed, "These men forsake the eternal world to live in the temporal world!" Whatever they looked at was immediately destroyed. A Divine voice then proclaimed, "Have you come out to destroy My world? Go back to your cave!"[14]

Upon leaving the cave the second time, the older, calmer R. Shimon learned his lesson. But the youthful, passionate Elazar had a harder time. "Whomever Rabbi Eleazer hurt, Rabbi Shimon would heal."[15] For Rabbi Elazar, the cave was still the ideal that the world did not live up to. Eventually, Rabbi Shimon succeeding in showing Rabbi Elazar that other ways of serving the Creator also have value.

On Erev Shabbat, as it was getting dark, they saw an old man running in the twilight holding two bunches of myrtles. When they asked him what they were for, he answered, "They are in honor of the Shabbat. One is for the commandment to 'remember' and one is for the commandment to 'observe.' Rabbi Shimon then said to his son, "See how precious the *mitzvot* are to Israel!" Their minds were then put at ease.[16]

His single-mindedness gone, Rabbi Elazar's focus began to reach beyond Torah. Now able to value the life of the working man, Rabbi Elazar became one himself – not a farmer working alone in field or brewer working

---

[14] See note 11 above.

[15] Ibid.

[16] Ibid.

in his brewery, but, of all professions, as a detective on the beat looking for thieves. What motivated Rabbi Elazar to abandon full-time Torah study to chase criminals? Well, he was very good at it. Some advice that he gave to a local detective reached the ears of the king, who appointed him as the local sleuth. Rabbi Elazar, once unable to fathom how people could think about this world at all, was now immersed in it, and his colleagues disapproved.[17] Not only was he working in a profession that they considered less than honorable, but he was working for the very same Roman government that had forced his father to hide in a cave for twelve years, in a similar role as his despised grandfather – as an informer arresting fellow Jews! This irony was not lost on his colleagues, who dubbed him "Vinegar, the son of Wine." If he had learned the lesson of being in the cave a little too strongly before, they must have thought, then perhaps he was learning the lesson of leaving the cave too strongly now. As for Rabbi Elazar, he was only doing what he felt was right: keeping criminals off the streets. When Rabbi Yehoshua (perhaps ben Levi) challenged him regarding how he could "deliver the people of our God up to the slaughter," Rabbi Elazar replied, "I simply weed out the thorns from the vineyard." Unimpressed, Rabbi Yehoshua answered, "Let the owner of the vineyard do it himself."[18]

The stress of the job, together with the abuse that he received from his colleagues, took its toll. The responsibility of apprehending criminals is a big one. It is even bigger when one is turning over one's fellow Jews to a foreign power. The fact that thieves were put to death under Roman law did not make it any easier.

As good as any individual is at his job, he is bound to make some mistakes. With the stakes so high, Rabbi Elazar could not forgive himself for making them. Once, he let his emotions get the better of him. When a local launderer insulted him, Rabbi Elazar arrested him on dubious charges. When

---

17 BT *Bava Metzia* 83b c. SA II:233.

18 Ibid.

he realized that he had made the arrest out of ulterior motives, he attempted to rescind his allegation, but it was too late. The system was already in motion. The launderer was put to death, and Rabbi Elazar went into a deep depression.[19]

Later on, Rabbi Elazar learned that he had in fact served as part of a Divine plan to punish the launderer for a crime that he had committed – raping an engaged woman on Yom Kippur! – but of which he had never been convicted. Although this knowledge gave Rabbi Elazar some comfort, he still could not forgive himself for having misused his power and causing a man's death without sufficient reason. Although miracles that were clear signs of Divine favor occurred in his life, showing that the Heavenly Court held him guiltless,[20] Rabbi Elazar was still guilty in his own eyes. He began to mutilate his body, perhaps in retribution for the launderer's body for whose destruction he felt responsible. With hyperbolic alliteration, the Midrash tells us:

> He invoked painful afflictions upon himself, so that although sixty sheets were spread under him in the evening, sixty basins of blood were removed from underneath him in the morning. Every morning his wife prepared a mixture of sixty kinds of fig pap for him, and when he ate it, he recovered. But she did not allow him to go to the yeshiva, since the scholars would cause him distress. In the evening Rabbi Elazar would invite the afflictions back…. One day his wife cried out, "So it is of your own volition that you bring these afflictions upon yourself, and to pay for your treatment you spend my family's money!" With that insult, she left her husband and went to her father's house. At that

---

[19] Ibid.

[20] Ibid.

35

moment, sixty sailors were sailing on the sea. When a huge wave crested over them, threatening to sink their ship, they cried out, "God of Elazar, save us!" The sea then calmed. When the sailors docked safely, they brought Rabbi Elazar a gift of sixty slaves holding sixty purses. The slaves prepared a mixture of sixty kinds of fig pap for him, which he ate.[21]

In the end, Rabbi Elazar recovered and forgave himself, and his wife returned to him. But as if his self-accusations had not been harmful enough, his colleagues' accusations were even worse. Upon his return to the Academy, his legal decisions were mocked. Once again miracles occurred, demonstrating Divine favor, but years of bitterness do not go away so quickly. The scholars could not forgive him for having worked as a detective.[22] His dying request to his wife was that she not bury him, but rather keep his body in the attic of their house because he did not want to have a funeral that none of the scholars would attend.[23]

If his contemporaries did not see his virtue, God certainly did. Although his body remained in the attic for more than eighteen years, miraculously it did not decompose. Throughout that time, no wild animal entered the town. The townspeople began coming to Rabbi Elazar's house to put their legal cases before the closed attic door, from behind which a voice would give a ruling. This situation might have continued indefinitely if Rabbi Shimon bar Yochai had not appeared to the scholars in a dream, insisting that they bury his son. In the end, the scholars buried Rabbi Elazar (much to the chagrin of his townspeople, who had gotten used to the

---

21 BT *Bava Metzia* 84b c. SA ibid.

22 Ibid.

23 Ibid.

benefits of having his corpse around),[24] giving him an appropriate eulogy as "a master of Tanach and Mishna, a poet and an orator."[25]

Thus Rabbi Elazar, who began by judging others so harshly, ended by being judged himself. In the end, the scholars learned the lesson that it had taken Rabbi Elazar so many years to learn: that one cannot judge another's religious commitment based on his profession, and that there are many ways to serve God including Torah study, honest work, and myrtle branches. While Rabbi Elazar's passion is praiseworthy, it was even more commendable when he could temper it and make room for others.

A postscript: A young man, the son of a great scholar, shows no interest in studying Torah. A great rabbi, confident that the son would follow in his father's footsteps if only he had the right training, takes him under his wing. Thus began the scholarly life of Yosi, the son Rabbi Elazar, the son of Rabbi Shimon bar Yochai.[26]

---

[24] Ibid.

[25] *Va-yikra Rabbah* 30:1 c. SA II:233.

[26] BT *Bava Metzia* 85a c. SA II:306.

RABBI ELIEZER BEN HYRCANUS

(First–second centuries CE[*])

Warm yourself by the fire of the scholars, but watch out for their glowing coals or you will be burnt because they bite like foxes, sting like scorpions, hiss like serpents, and all their words are like burning hot coals.[1]

THIS IS NOT the sort of pronouncement that one would expect from one of the greatest scholars of his generation, a man who served as their representative before the Romans,[2] presided over the greatest rabbinical court of his time,[3] and brother in law of Rabban Gamliel, the most aristocratic of all the scholars.[4] A man of whom his teacher said, "If all of the scholars were on one side of a scale and Eliezer ben Hyrcanus was on the other side, he would outweigh them all."[5] How can Rabbi Eliezer, who

---

[*] If we take literally the tradition that Rabbi Akiva lived for 120 years (see the chapter on Rabbi Akiva above, n. 1), Rabbi Eliezer could not have been born after the year 30 since he was already a well-known scholar when Rabbi Akiva went to study with him (see chapter on Rabbi Akiva, n. 27). This would have to have been the year 55 at the earliest (see chapter on Rabbi Akiva, n. 1), after Rabbi Eliezer had studied with Rabbi Yohanan ben Zakkai for three years, beginning at age 22 (n. 7). The latest that he could have died is the year 135, since his death preceded that of Rabbi Akiva (n. 33).

[1] Mishna, *Avot* 2:10.

[2] JT *Sanhedrin* 7:16.

[3] BT *Sanhedrin* 32b.

[4] BT *Shabbat* 116a. See chapter on Rabban Gamliel.

[5] Mishna *Avot* 2:8.

seems to be the scholar *par excellence*, make such harsh statements about himself and his contemporaries?

Eliezer ben Hyrcanus was not truly one the scholars. Regardless of how much prestige he had, irrespective of how many students came to learn from him, he was always an outsider looking in. From the beginning, he lacked the background to be part of the culture of the scholars, and until his dying day he never fit in. "Watch out for the fire of the scholars," he said – the fire to which he had gone in the hope of getting warm and ended up getting burnt.

His father, Hyrcanus, was a simple farmer who could not perceive the genius that his son possessed. For Hyrcanus, a man's job was to work the field. He felt that while other pursuits might have value, they were not for any of his sons to try. Eliezer's brothers agreed with him. However, Eliezer was unique and sought something beyond the fields. This was something Hyrcanus could not understand.

> One day Rabbi Eliezer's brothers were plowing arable ground while he was plowing a stony plot on a hill. He sat down and began to cry.
>
> His father asked, "Why are you crying? Are you upset because you have to plow a stony plot? For now on, you may plow arable land." But on the arable land he again sat down and began to cry.
>
> His father asked, "Why are you weeping? Are you upset that you are plowing arable ground?"
>
> "No."
>
> "Then why are you crying?"
>
> "Because I want to study Torah."
>
> "You are twenty-two already, and you want to start studying Torah? Get married, have children, and they can study."[6]

---

[6] *Pirke de-Rabbi Eliezer* 1:1–2 c. SA II:88.

What more can there be to life than cultivating your garden? But Eliezer was already far away from tilling the soil. He wanted to struggle in the world of Torah.

As has happened since the beginning of time, Eliezer's relationship with his father deteriorated from bad communication to outright rebellion. A father can keep his son under his control as long as the son complies, but at twenty-two years old,[7] Eliezer stopped complying. Taking an injury to his heifer as a sign that he should leave the field, he fled to the center of the Torah world, the metropolis of Jerusalem.[8]

He was not prepared for his impulsive flight. He starved on his journey, with a clod of earth as his only nourishment[9] (or, as some traditions have it, a clod of cow dung[10]). Famished but determined, he arrived in Jerusalem. He walked straight into the academy of Rabbi Yohanan ben Zakkai, and upon meeting the great scholar, broke down.

> "Why are you crying?" the rabbi asked him.
> "Because I want to study Torah."
> "You have never studied it?"
> "No."
> So Rabbi Yochanan began to teach him the *shema*, *birkat ha-mazon* and two *halakhot* every day. On Shabbat, Rabbi Eliezer repeated the prayers and the *halakhot* until he had them memorized.[11]

---

[7] *Avot de-Rabbi Natan,* Chapter 6 c. SA ibid.

[8] *Bereshit Rabbah* 42:1 c. SA ibid.

[9] Ibid.

[10] See n. 7 above.

[11] *Pirke de-Rabbi Eliezer* 1:3–4 c. SA ibid.

Eliezer was determined not only to learn but also to fit in, not to look like an outsider. How else can we explain his going to the academy each day during his first eight days in Jerusalem without mentioning to anyone that had nothing to eat? While the other students were being supported by their proud parents, who were hoping that their children would be the future teachers of Torah, Eliezer was alone, practically disowned, in a strange city. To mention this to his colleagues, and particularly to his teacher, would have drawn attention to the fact that he was only an unlettered farmer, the son of an unlettered farmer, and not a sophisticated cosmopolitan as they were, studying Bible at five and Mishna at ten.

Soon his cover was blown. All the lies in the world cannot cover up bad breath.

> Rabbi Yohanan knew that his bad breath was not from something rotten in his mouth, but rather because he had nothing to eat.[12]
> Rabbi Yohanan said to Eliezer, "You will eat with me."
> He responded, "I have already eaten at the place where I am staying."
> Rabbi Yochanan then told his students to bring Eliezer's innkeepers to him.
> He asked them, "Did Eliezer eat with you today?"
> They answered, "No."
> That is how they realized that he had had nothing to eat for eight days.[13]

Poor man! He even tried to hide his circumstances from his landlord. Even sadder, he failed.

---

[12] *Midrash Tanhuma* (ed. Buber), Lech Lecha 10 c. SA ibid.

[13] *Pirke de-Rabbi Eliezer* 1:5–6 c. SA ibid.

It was then that his fortunes changed, for Rabbi Yohanan had no interest in money or pedigree, but only in his student's desire to learn. He also had a sense of humor about the situation. He said, "Just as bad breath rose out of your mouth reached me, so too the fragrance of Torah rising out of your mouth will reach the whole world."[14]

From that point on, Rabbi Yohanan gave him not only *halakhot*, but square meals as well.[15]

For the next three years, Eliezer sat at the feet of Rabbi Yohanan.[16] Although he learned a great deal, he displayed a lack of confidence in his ability in his own creativity. Though he mastered all that he was taught by his teacher, he was unable to strike out on his own and develop his own ideas. He refused to speak publicly, telling Rabbi Yohanan, "Just as a well cannot produce any more water than falls into it, I cannot say any more Torah than what I have received from you." Though Rabbi Yohanan responded that Eliezer is "like a spring, which wells up and brings water of itself,"[17] except for one flash of brilliance, which burst forth as he delivered a discourse before his father (thus finally winning his respect),[18] there were no further bursts of creativity. In the end, Rabbi Yohanan had to admit that Eliezer is rather "like a plastered cistern that does not lose a drop, like a flask covered with pitch which retains its wine," while the attribute of "a spring that which constantly strengthens itself " was bestowed upon another of his students, Elazar ben Arach.[19]

---

[14] *Bereshit Rabba* 42:1, *Pirkei de-Rabbi Eliezer* 1:5 c. SA ibid.

[15] See n. 12.

[16] Ibid.

[17] *Pirke de-Rabbi Eliezer* Chapter II c. S.A. ibid.

[18] Ibid.

[19] See n. 5, SA II:89.

As Rabbi Eliezer's awe of his teachers and the knowledge that he gained from them grew, his confidence in his own ability diminished. Disciples coming to hear Rabbi Eliezer's Torah were sorely disappointed.

> Rabbi Eliezer was spending Shabbat in the Upper Galilee, and he was asked about thirty *halakhot* of a sukkah. Regarding twelve of them he said, "I heard the law from my teachers," and regarding the remaining eighteen he said, "I have not heard the law from my teachers."
>
> He was asked, "Master, do you say anything other than what you have heard?"
>
> He replied, "I have never in my life said anything that I had not heard from my teachers."[20]

R. Eliezer even avoided answering the simplest questions, unwilling to risk saying something that might be his original interpretation. Another question regarding the laws of a sukkah led to this absurd dialogue:

> Rabbi Yohanan ben Ilai asked Rabbi Eliezer, "May one spread a cloth over the top of a sukkah to increase the amount of shade?"
>
> Rabbi Eliezer responded, "There was not a tribe in Israel that did not produce a judge."
>
> Rabbi Yohanan repeated, "May one spread a cloth over the top of a sukkah to increase the amount of shade?"
>
> Rabbi Eliezer responded, "There was not a tribe in Israel that did not produce any prophets, and the tribes of Yehudah and Binyamin appointed their kings at the request of their prophets."

---

[20] BT *Sukkah* 28a c. SA II:92.

This could have gone on forever had the frustrated questioner not given up, finally covering the sukkah with a cloth. Rabbi Eliezer showed his disapproval by then leaving the sukkah, thus sticking to his principle of not saying anything that he had not heard from his teachers that might be a product of his own original thinking.[21]

What caused Rabbi Eliezer's resistance to any innovation? We can conjecture based on what we know. Eliezer arrived in Jerusalem as an illiterate farmhand, completely uneducated not only in Torah but also in the urban culture of Jerusalem, to the point that he chose to starve rather than expose his profound social ignorance, which was clear to any Jerusalemite who saw him. To compensate for the insecurity that he felt as an outsider, he learned Torah with unparalleled passion ("All my life no one arrived at the study hall earlier or left later than I did"[22]). While he could learn Torah through hard work and study, the unwritten rules of the cosmopolitan society in which he lived were inaccessible to him. His own personality, ideas and desires were suppressed, covered over by thousands of *halakhot* that did not originate with an ignorant farm boy, but with the most respected man in Jerusalem, Rabbi Yohanan. For him it is not the individual who matters, but rather the traditions that he possesses. In Rabbi Eliezer's world, "One who says something that he did not hear from his teacher causes the Divine Presence to depart from Israel."[23] Likewise, "A disciple who teaches in front of his own teacher deserves death."[24] Thus he could be a part of this Jerusalem that he could never fit into, for he was no longer Eliezer the son of Hyrcanus, but the greatest student of Rabbi Yohanan.

---

[21] BT *Sukkah* 27b c. SA II:93.

[22] See n. 20.

[23] BT *Berachot* 27b.

[24] JT *Gittin* 1:2, *Va-yikra Rabbah* 20:6 c. SA II:95.

Rabbi Eliezer's unbreakable loyalty to the traditions that he learned can be seen in this disturbing story. A servant of Rabbi Eliezer passed away. She was a woman who had lived in his house, served him, and was undoubtedly part of his life. His students all came to his house in order to console him in his grief on losing someone who was certainly very dear to him. When they entered his house, he went upstairs. When they followed him upstairs, he went into the bathroom. When they went into the bathroom, he went into the dining room. Finally, Rabbi Eliezer turned angrily to his students, reprimanding them for coming to console him, for according to *halakha,* one does not mourn the death of a servant.[25] Rabbi Eliezer once again pushed away his own humanity, replacing it with the halakha as he learned it from his teachers.

Then, one day, it all came crashing down. The conflict between Rabbi Eliezer's learning and the culture of the sages finally came to a head, and Rabbi Eliezer lost. Here is how it happened.

It was a regular day at the academy. A discussion ensued as to whether or not a certain make of oven is susceptible to becoming ritually impure. Rabbi Eliezer took one side while all the scholars took the other. Rabbi Eliezer knew that he was right, but the crowd rejected his arguments one by one. He was one man against the many, fighting for the truth. Finally he abandons all rational arguments, appealing to Nature itself to come to his aid. A carob tree walked off and replanted itself and a river flowed backward, all in testament to the truth of Rabbi Eliezer's position. "What does it matter?" the scholars answered. "We do not learn halakha from carob trees or rivers." Rabbi Eliezer called out to the walls of the yeshiva, which have heard more Torah than any human being, inside which Rabbi Eliezer spent endless hours studying. The walls, seeing their hero being vanquished in their midst, begin to collapse. But then they stop falling after being reminded by the scholars that the Torah is decided by humans, not by walls. Finally,

---

[25] BT *Berachot* 16b c. SA II:97. In the Talmud this behavior is contrasted with that of Rabbi Gamliel, who found a reason to allow mourning for his servant.

with no other recourse, Rabbi Eliezer calls out to God Himself to support his position, which God does, until He too is reminded by the scholars that the Torah is "not in heaven," but given to human beings to decide.[26] And the Torah taught us that we do not appeal to God to decide matters. We follow the human majority, not claims of objective truth stated by individuals, no matter how wise they may be. The Torah does not consist only in the memorization of *halakhot* but is found in the life of the Jewish people, which includes many scholars, not just the greatest one of each generation. When the majority decides and the people follow that ruling, that is the Torah, regardless of any intellectual proof that could be brought.

All of this flies in the face of everything Rabbi Eliezer believed. If it is true that the Torah is as much of a culture as it is a set of objective rules from heaven, then how can a farmhand with no knowledge of that culture play such an important role? It is hard work and a passion for the truth that make a scholar, and nothing else. Eliezer worked harder than anyone else, and as God Himself attested, he found the truth.

But it is useless to fight the existing social order, and the one cannot defeat the many.

> On that day, anything that Rabbi Eliezer had declared pure was burned.... The scholars then took a vote and excommunicated Rabbi Eliezer.[27]

From then on, Rabbi Eliezer lived in a state of bitterness. Nothing is more frustrating for a teacher than to be without students. He said, "I have studied three hundred *halakhot* about *tzara'at*, and three hundred *halakhot* about growing cucumbers (some say three thousand), yet no one has ever

---

[26] BT *Bava Metzia* 59a–b c. SA II:98.

[27] BT ibid. 59b, c. SA ibid.

asked me about them."[28] His bitterness knew no bounds. Even Nature itself was affected.

> As tears streamed down his eyes, the world was smitten. A third of the olive, wheat, and barley crops were ruined. Some say that even the dough in women's hands spoiled.[29]

Rabban Gamliel, his brother-in-law and head of the academy, was found dead. It happened at the moment when Rabbi Eliezer was praying.[30]

Some time later, as Rabbi Eliezer approached death, describing himself as a "Torah scroll about to be rolled up," several of his peers finally came to learn from him.[31] Still, they took care to sit four cubits away from him, the distance that one is required to keep from someone under a ban.[32] They asked him to teach them Torah, but from Rabbi Eliezer's perspective, it was already too late.

> "I am concerned that perhaps that the scholars of this generation will be punished with death."
> "For what?"
> "Since they did not come to learn from me."[33]

Here the scholars gave him one last chance to reassess his opposing positions, asking for one last time his opinion on questions of ritual purity in which he disagreed with the scholars. But even then he would not give in and kept to the positions that he had articulated years before.[34] Now, in his

---

[28] BT *Sanhedrin* 68a and JT *Shabbat* 2:7, c. SA II:102.

[29] See n. 17 above.

[30] Ibid.

[31] See n. 28.

[32] *Avot de-Rabbi Natan*, chapter 25.

[33] Ibid.

[34] BT Sanhedrin 68 with Rashi ad loc.

final moments, there was yet another sign from God that demonstrated his Maker's approval.

> The last thing he said was "Pure." They said, "This proves that he was pure."

This time the rabbis accepted God's testimony and declared: "The ban is lifted! The ban is lifted! He is our father, the horseman and chariot of Israel!"[35]

---

[35] See n. 28.

ELISHA BEN AVUYAH

(First–second centuries CE)[*]

One who studies Torah as a child, to what is he compared? To ink written on fresh paper. One who studies Torah as an old man, to what is he compared? To ink written on blotted paper.[1]

ELISHA BEN AVUYAH IS NOT as well known for being a scholar as he is for being a heretic. Once a respected scholar, he left the fold and stopped observing the Torah and thereafter was called by the name Aher, "Another."[2] Elisha's story is filled with questions. What made him leave everything that he knew for another lifestyle? Why, after having left the world of the scholars, did he continue to teach Torah to Rabbi Meir, even cautioning him against violating rabbinic rulings?[3] If he still cared about Judaism, as his interaction with Rabbi Meir would seem to imply, why did he not return to it?

The various reasons given seem too superficial to explain such a radical break. According to one account, when he witnessed the deaths of various people while they were performing *mitzvot*, he found this so unbearable that he left Judaism.[4] Other accounts, such as the following one, mention his connection to Greek culture:

---

[*] Born before the destruction of Jerusalem in the year 70 (see n. 6).

[1] Mishna *Avot* 4:20.

[2] BT *Hagigah* 15a c. SA II:191.

[3] BT *Hagigah,* ibid; JT *Hagigah* 2:1,*Ruth Rabbah* 6:2, *Kohelet Rabbah* 7:16 c. SA ibid.

[4] BT *Hullin* 142a, BT *Kiddushin* 39b, JT *Hagigah* ibid; *Ruth Rabbah* ibid.; *Kohelet Rabbah* ibid. c. SA ibid.

Greek song was always in his mouth, and whenever he rose to leave the house of study, many heretical books would fall from his lap.[5]

It takes more than a challenging philosophical problem or a purely intellectual interest in foreign ideas to reject one's own people and therefore be rejected by them, to lose one's family and friends and to give up one's stability and place in the world. Therefore, if we look at Elisha's own version of the road to his apostasy, we are likely to be disappointed by its lack of persuasion.

Avuyah, my father, was a well-respected man in Jerusalem. When he was arranging my *brit milah*, he invited all the well-known people of Jerusalem. Among them were Rabbi Eliezer and Rabbi Yehoshua. After the guests had eaten and drunk, they began to clap their hands and dance. Some sang songs, while others composed poetry. Rabbi Eliezer said to Rabbi Yehoshua, "They are doing what interests them. Let us do what interests us." They began to study the Torah, then the Prophets, then the Writings. A pillar of fire then came down from the sky and surrounded them. Avuyah said to them, "My masters, have you come here to set my house on fire?" They replied, "God forbid! We were merely learning Torah, and as the Torah was as joyful as when it was originally given at Sinai, it accompanied itself by fire as at Sinai." Elated, my father Avuyah said, "My masters, since the power of Torah is so great, I will dedicate this child to its study."

---

[5] BT *Hagigah* 15b c. SA ibid.

But since my father's intentions were not for the sake of Heaven, my study of Torah did not last.[6]

This is yet another explanation that does not reach the depth of the problem. What do a father's ulterior motives have to do with a grown man's apostasy?

Even more difficult to understand is why Elisha did not repent. The reason given is that he did not believe that he could, as he said:

I was riding a horse behind the academy on a Yom Kippur that fell on Shabbat, and I heard a Divine voice saying, "Return, backsliding children! Return to Me and I will return to you – except for Aher."[7]

The incident that put the final, irrevocable seal on Aher's decision never to return is odder still.

Aher said to a child, "Tell me what verse you have learned." The child answered, "God says to the wicked: 'What right do you have to recite My laws?'" But since the child had a speech impediment, his words sounded like: "God said to Elisha…."

Thus Elisha was thoroughly convinced that God had rejected him and that he was doomed to live as a heretic. [8]

There can be no understanding Aher, the scholar turned scorner, without realizing the importance in his life of Rabbi Akiva, the scorner

---

[6] JT *Hagigah* ibid; *Ruth Rabbah* 6:2, *Kohelet Rabbah* ibid. c. SA ibid.

[7] BT *Hagigah* 15a, JT *Hagigah* ibid. c. SA ibid.

[8] BT *Hagigah* 15a–b c. SA ibid. Here the Talmud cites one opinion that he murdered the child, though that tradition is contested.

turned scholar. Together, they undertook the "journey into the Orchard," a mystical encounter from which Rabbi Akiva "emerged unharmed," but during which Elisha "mutilated the shoots" and left as a heretic.[9] Elisha continued to teach Rabbi Meir the teachings of Rabbi Akiva after his apostasy.[10] For although Elisha was a scholar, his world view was diametrically opposed to that of Rabbi Akiva, and this is what sent him irreversibly down the wrong path.

One teaching particularly illustrates this point. One Shabbat, Elisha (now Aher) was riding on horseback, in violation of the rabbinic ruling. Hearing that his teacher was outside, Rabbi Meir left his lecturing to run outside and learn from him. After hearing Rabbi Meir's interpretation of a certain verse, Elisha then told him how Rabbi Akiva would have taught it:

> As vessels of gold and even vessels of glass can be repaired if broken, so can a scholar recover his learning after he has lost it.[11]

This teaching is consistent with Rabbi Akiva's optimistic view of the world. One can accomplish anything if one works at it. Human beings are always given the choice and they can always improve, no matter what their past. Rabbi Akiva, who began his life as an ignorant shepherd and became a great scholar, was living proof of this teaching.

However, during his life as a scholar, Elisha understood the verse much differently.

> The Torah is as difficult to acquire as golden vessels and as easy to lose as glass vessels.... For although golden vessels

---

[9] BT *Hagigah* 14b, JT *Hagigah* ibid.

[10] BT *Hagigah* 15a; JT *Hagigah* ibid; *Ruth Rabbah* ibid; *Kohelet Rabbah* ibid. c. SA ibid.

[11] BT *Hagigah* ibid; JT *Hagigah* ibid; *Ruth Rabbah* ibid. c. SA ibid.

may be repaired after they break, glass vessels can never be repaired.[12]

What is lost is lost forever, and no amount of hoping or working can ever bring it back. This is the point of departure between Elisha and Rabbi Akiva, and it leads down radically different paths. While Akiva was confident that he could rise as high as he was able regardless of his humble background, Elisha believed that he could do nothing to avoid his fate as a rejected heretic. Let us look at Elisha's most famous teaching:

> One who studies Torah as a child, to what is he compared? To ink written on fresh paper. One who studies Torah as an old man, to what is he compared? To ink written on blotted paper.[13]

Can anything be more foreign to the mindset of Rabbi Akiva – who only began to read at the age of forty – than this?

Rabbi Akiva and Elisha ben Avuyah lived during difficult times. The Holy Temple was in ruins. The Bar Kokhba revolt, which had begun with so much promise, ended in failure. Roman persecution was unforgiving, and the Jewish people watched helplessly as its teachers were murdered one by one. Elisha himself "saw the tongue of Hutzpit the Translator [or Yaakov the Baker, or both] being dragged in the dirt by a swine."[14]

Yet although Rabbi Akiva and Elisha witnessed the same events, their perceptions were radically different. Rabbi Akiva, the optimist, saw all this as a transitory hardship that paved the way for redemption. He felt that no problem was insurmountable and that any hardship could be overcome,

---

[12] *Avot de-Rabbi Natan,* Chapter 24.

[13] See n. 1.

[14] See n. 4 above.

since "whatever God does is for the best."[15] This teaching of Rabbi Akiva, which Elisha understood as the essence of Judaism, Elisha first questioned, then rejected, then abhorred. Not only could damage never be undone, he maintained, but there is no Divine plan ensuring a positive end. If things are bad, it is because they are doomed to be so, and no amount of optimism can change that. Like the Fatalist philosophers whose works he presumably read, Elisha could find no meaning in all the suffering. For him, it was inevitable: the world continues on its callous course, and anything human beings do to change it is futile. Elisha thus saw his own life on a meaningless, unalterable path that, from infancy, doomed him to apostasy with no hope of repentance. This is the reason for his fascination with Rabbi Akiva's teachings. Rabbi Akiva's hope, optimism, and belief in the power within every human being and the entire world to change for the better represented the Judaism that Elisha rejected. This is what he taught Rabbi Meir, knowing full well that he himself could never believe it.

But in the end, history proved him wrong. Rabbi Akiva was correct in his belief that no matter how bad things may appear, we must believe that they will work out ultimately for the best. The Jewish people not only lived on, but Elisha's own grandchildren were also among its leaders. As the Talmud says:

> Had Aher known the interpretation of a verse given by Rabbi Yaakov, his daughter's son, he would not have sinned.[16]

---

[15] BT *Berachot* 60b c. SA II:166, see chapter on Rabbi Akiva above.

[16] BT *Kiddushin* ibid; BT *Hullin* ibid. (translation from *Encyclopaedia Judaica*).

RABBAN GAMLIEL OF YAVNEH[1]

(First–second centuries CE)*

Lord of the Universe! You know full well that I have not acted in this way for my honor, nor for my family's honor, but for Your honor, so that strife may not multiply in Israel.[2]

THE DEMOCRATIC SPIRIT is the lifeblood of talmudic debate. The right to put forward an idea is not related to its presenter's profession, family, or political power. Only one criterion – whether or not the speaker knows what he is talking about – is taken into account.

However, there was one exception. During his tenure as Head of the Academy, Rabban Gamliel of Yavneh instituted a policy of silencing dissenting voices. This raises a question regarding how the talmudic tradition can pay such a great deal of respect to someone who went against its most basic convention.

Rabban Gamliel was the leader of the Jewish people during a turbulent time in its history, succeeding his father Rabbi Shimon ben

---

[1] 1 Known in scholarship as Gamliel II. Not to be confused with his grandfather, Rabban Gamliel the Elder (or Gamliel I). The differentiating appendage "of Yavneh" is found in *Mahzor Vitry* 424, s.v. *"Moshe kibel."* The *Encyclopaedia Judaica* lists another four Gamliels who were subsequently born to his family line.

* Rabban Gamliel served as the second *nasi* after the destruction of the Bet ha-Mikdash in the year 68 CE (n. 3). He died before Rabbi Eliezer ben Hyrcanus (see chapter on Rabbi Eliezer ben Hyrcanus above, n. 30) which was before 135 (see note 1 above, ibid.).

[2] BT *Bava Metzia* 59b c. SA II:98.

Gamliel and Rabbi Yohanan ben Zakkai as the Head of the Academy at Yavneh.[3] Before him, Rabbis Shimon and Yohanan were faced with a challenge that must have seemed insurmountable: to reframe the Jewish religious experience in light of the recent destruction of the Temple (Bet ha-Mikdash) in Jerusalem. Although this was not a simple matter, it was necessary. The Temple had been the center of Jewish life. Approximately half of the Tannaitic laws discussed issues related to the Temple.[4] The pilgrimages to Jerusalem were the major cultural and religious events of the year. The Sanhedrin, or High Court, sat on the Temple Mount, thus making Jerusalem the legal center as well. Suddenly, all this changed. As Jerusalem was besieged by the Romans, Rabbi Yohanan made a fateful decision to give up the capital and asked Vespasian, the Roman general commanding the siege, for only three things: a doctor to treat Rav Tzadok (who was suffering from complications due to starvation), that the city of Yavneh and the scholars who were living there be spared, and that the dynasty of Rabban Gamliel the Elder be protected.[5]

As the high court relocated from the capital of Jerusalem to the small settlement of Yavneh, it was up to its heads, Rabbis Yohanan and Shimon, to chart the course for the newly challenged religion. Mostly on the initiative of Rabbi Yohanan, they undertook to adjust Jewish philosophy and ritual to the new reality, all without losing the ideal of the Temple as a central concept in an ideal state.

---

[3] The term "Head of the Academy" is the name of his title in BT *Berakhot* 27b (c. SA II: 75). Rashi (ad loc. and in BT *Sanhedrin* 11b) identifies this position as that of the *nasi*. It seems from *Midrash Tannaim,* Devarim 26:14, that Rabbis Yohanan and Shimon filled the same function.

[4] Of the six orders of the Mishna, two and a half – Kodashim, Taharot, and half of Mo'ed – are dedicated to issues relating to sacrifices, the Temple service, and ritual purity.

[5] BT *Gittin* 56b according to Rashi ad loc. c. SA I:2:2.

> Once when Rabbi Yohanan ben Zakkai was leaving Jerusalem, Rabbi Yehoshua was walking behind him and saw the Temple in ruins. Rabbi Yehoshua said, "Woe to us that this has been destroyed, the place where atonement was made for the sins of Israel."
>
> He answered, "No, my son, do you not know that we have another means of atonement? These are acts of loving kindness, as it is written, "'I desire kindness, not sacrifices.'"[6]

Similarly,

> Rabbi Yohanan explained that as long as the Temple stood, the altar atoned for Israel, but now the way a man behaves at his own table atones for him.[7]

Rabbis Shimon and Yohanan taught that although the Temple was no longer standing, people still could relate to God in other ways. This approach was not limited to philosophy, but led to halakhic adaptations as well. When the Temple was standing and Rosh ha-Shannah fell on Shabbat, the shofar would only be blown within its confines. Now it would be blown "anywhere that there was a High Court."[8] When the Temple was standing, one would shake the Four Species only there throughout the entire Sukkot festival, while only on the first day outside of its confines. Now the Four Species were shaken on all seven days (excluding Shabbat), no matter where Jews lived, "in memory of the Temple."[9] The time frame for accepting witnesses for Rosh Hodesh was lengthened because intricacies related to the

---

[6] *Avot de-Rabbi Natan,* Chapter 4.

[7] BT *Berakhot* 55a.

[8] Mishna *Rosh Hashannah* 4:1.

[9] Ibid. 4:3.

Temple law were no longer a concern.[10] In order to ensure stability, the halakhic positions of Bet Hillel were adopted, with the accompanying command: "Anyone who violates the positions of Beit Hillel shall be punished with death."[11]

During a period of upheaval, the leaders of the High Court had the courage to redefine many essential aspects of Jewish life. Whether or not this adapted form of the ancient religion would persevere or not was left to their successor, Rabban Gamliel of Yavneh.

For his part, Rabban Gamliel continued in the same manner as his predecessors. He emphasized the importance of speaking about the Pesah sacrifice at the seder,[12] since it was no longer performed as there was no access to the Temple Mount. He instituted three mandatory daily prayers,[13] the number of blessings that they must contain (eighteen),[14] and helped establish the times that they must be recited,[15] since prayer now had to replace the sacrificial service.[16]

Nevertheless, the national upheaval was still too recent for comfort. Feeling that any controversy might damage the recently adopted path, Rabban Gamliel actively shut out all dissent.

> This is how Rabban Gamliel conducted himself: When he walked into the academy and asked if there were any questions, it was because he was told beforehand that there would not be any. If he entered and did not ask if there were

---

[10] Ibid. 4:4.

[11] JT *Yevamot* 1:6.

[12] Mishna *Pesahim* 10:5.

[13] BT *Berakhot* 27b.

[14] Ibid. 28b.

[15] Mishna *Berakhot* 1:1.

[16] BT *Berakhot* 26b.

any questions, it was because he was told beforehand that there would be.[17]

Rabban Gamliel's unwillingness to tolerate any dissent was so great that he even played a central role in the excommunication of his own brother-in-law, Rabbi Eliezer ben Hyrcanus, who held an alternate view regarding the ritual purity of a certain oven.[18] Yet intelligent and sensitive people will not tolerate autocrats for long, and eventually Rabban Gamliel's methods were challenged in a series of conflicts with Rabbi Yehoshua ben Hananiah.

The first conflict revolved around the acceptance of testimony regarding when the new moon was first seen, thus beginning the new month. This is a critical issue, since the determination of a new month directly affects the date on which the festivals will be celebrated.

> Two witnesses came to the High Court and testified, "We saw the new moon at its proper time, but on the next night when there should have been a moon, there was none." Rabban Gamliel accepted their evidence [regardless of its logical inconsistency], but Rabbi Dosa ben Harkinas said, "They are false witnesses." Rabbi Yehoshua said to Rabbi Dosa: I agree with your position."
>
> Rabban Gamliel then sent Rabbi Yehoshua a message: I request that you appear before me with your staff and your money on the day that you have determined to be Yom Kippur.

---

[17] Sifre *Devarim* 16 c. SA II:76.

[18] See note 1 and chapter on Rabbi Eliezer ben Hyrcanus above.

It was not sufficient for Rabban Gamliel to oppose Rabbi Yehoshua or even establish the halakha contrary to his opinion. He forced Rabbi Yehoshua to violate the day that he had determined would be Yom Kippur as a public admission of his guilt. Still, the scholars gave Rabban Gamliel the benefit of the doubt, feeling that this was the proper course to take in order to avoid halakhic chaos.

> Rabbi Akiva went to Rabbi Yehoshua and found him in great distress. He said to him, "I can prove that whatever Rabban Gamliel has done is valid, because the Torah says, 'These are the holy days of the Lord… which you shall proclaim,' which means 'Whether at their correct time or not, I only have these holidays.'" Rabbi Yehoshua then went to Rabbi Dosa ben Harkinas, who said to him, "If we question the calendar of the High Court of Rabban Gamliel, we must question the calendar of every High Court that has existed since the days of Moshe until the present."

With assurance from his colleagues that obedience to the High Court was the proper course of action, Rabbi Yehoshua accepted Rabban Gamliel's decree, and "took his staff and his money and went to Yavneh on the day that he thought was Yom Kippur."

Thus the episode ended peacefully when

> Rabban Gamliel rose and kissed him on his head and said, "Come in peace, my teacher and my disciple: my teacher in wisdom, and my disciple in that you have accepted my decision."[19]

---

[19] Mishna *Rosh Hashannah* 2:8–9 c. SA II:73.

However, this episode took its toll on Rabban Gamliel's reputation. For while he had accomplished his goal of silencing the opposition of Rabbi Yehoshua, who would now be hesitant to publicly speak against Rabban Gamliel again, some scholars felt offended on behalf of their colleague. The next incident illustrates their suspicion of Rabban Gamliel's motives.

Rabbi Tzadok had a question regarding the status of a first-born sheep of his, whether it was considered consecrated despite a minor blemish. In an ordinary case it would be considered consecrated, since we would suspect that the owner purposely injured it with the intention of changing its status to unconsecrated, but Rabbi Tzadok sought an exemption on the grounds that someone with his education would know that this was illegal and therefore be trusted not to injure the animal. He went to Rabbi Yehoshua, who indeed ruled that the animal is no longer considered consecrated, since there is a difference between a "knowledgeable kohen" and an "ignorant kohen." Rabbi Tzadok then asked Rabbi Gamliel, who ruled that no such distinction should be made. When he was told that Rabbi Yehoshua had ruled differently, Rabban Gamliel planned to crush Rabbi Yehoshua's dissent. He had the question asked in the Academy so that he could bring Rabbi Yehoshua's opposition out into the open. Rabbi Yehoshua, however, had learned his lesson from the new moon controversy.

> When they entered the Academy, the questioner arose and asked, "Is there any difference between an educated kohen and an ignorant one?"
> R. Yehoshua replied, "No."
> Rabban Gamliel then said, "Was it not told to me in your name that the answer was 'yes'? Yehoshua, stand up."
> Rabbi Yehoshua rose to his feet, and Rabban Gamliel continued sitting and lecturing.

If the scholars had supported Rabban Gamliel in the previous confrontation, they were not going to allow him to embarrass Rabbi Yehoshua again.

> While Rabbi Yehoshua stood, all the people murmured and eventually said to Hutzpit the interpreter [who expounded the ideas of the teacher], "Be quiet!" Hutzpit was then quiet.[20]

While mutiny was brewing, Rabban Gamliel continued with his tactic of crushing the opposition, which for the third time was Rabbi Yehoshua.

> It is related that a certain disciple came before Rabbi Yehoshua and asked him, "Is the evening tefillah obligatory or optional?"
> He replied, "It is optional."
> The disciple then presented himself before Rabban Gamliel and asked him, "Is the evening tefillah obligatory or optional?"
> He replied, "It is obligatory."
> "But," he said, "did Rabbi Yehoshua not tell me that it is optional?"
> He said, "Wait until the scholars enter the Academy."
> When the scholars came in, someone rose and asked, "Is the evening tefillah obligatory or optional?"
> Rabban Gamliel replied, "It is obligatory. Is there anyone who disputes this?"
> R. Yehoshua replied, "No."

---

[20] BT *Bekhorot* 36a c. SA II:74.

He said to him, "Did they not tell me that you said that it is optional? Yehoshua, stand up on your feet and let them testify against you!"

Rabban Gamliel remained sitting and expounding while Rabbi Yehoshua remained standing.

This time, the scholars had had enough.

All the people there began to shout to Hutzpit the interpreter, 'Stop!' and he stopped. They then said, "How long is Rabban Gamliel to go on insulting Rabbi Yehoshua? On New Year last year he insulted him, he insulted him in the matter of the firstborn in the affair of Rabbi Tzadok, and now he insults him again! Come, let us depose him!"

Rabbi Gamliel had gone too far. He was replaced as Head of the Academy by Rabbi Elazar ben Azariah, who was eighteen years old.

A new democratic spirit entered the Academy.

On that day the doorkeeper was removed and permission was given to all students to enter, as Rabban Gamliel previously decreed that no student who is insincere could enter the Academy. On that day many benches were added. Rabbi Yohanan said, "There is a difference of opinion on this matter between Abba Yoseph ben Dostai and the rabbis — one says that four hundred stools were added, and the other says seven hundred."

Rabban Gamliel became alarmed and said, "Perhaps, God forbid, I withheld Torah from Israel!" He was shown in his dream white casks full of ashes [symbolizing that the increase in Torah study was only superficial].[21] However, it meant nothing – he was only shown it so that he would be placated.

There was no halakha about which any doubt existed in the Academy that was not fully elucidated on that day.[22]

What motivated Rabban Gamliel to act in the autocratic manner that ultimately led to his downfall? One can conjecture that it was his own pride. This seems to be the view of one talmudic narrative, which qualifies a claim that Rabban Gamliel was modest by explaining:

It is possible that the modesty shown by Rabban Gamliel in this case belongs to the period after he had been deposed.[23]

Another conjecture judges Rabban Gamliel much more favorably. When Jerusalem fell, his family was preserved to carry out the vital mission of ensuring a viable future for the Jewish religion. As an embattled leader in a time of crisis, Rabban Gamliel saw no other way to maintain order than to silence the opposition. True, Judaism believes in listening to multiple voices, but no voice will be heard at all if Judaism does not survive. One could claim that it was not Rabban Gamliel's self-importance that dictated his policies, but rather his concern for the larger public.

This is the view that God Himself took in a story that took place in the aftermath of the excommunication of Rabbi Eliezer ben Hyrcanus.

Rabban Gamliel was traveling in a ship when a huge wave arose to drown him.

"It appears to me," he reflected, "that this is on account of excommunicating Rabbi Eliezer ben Hyrcanus."

[21] Rashi *Berakhot* 28a s.v., *"dimalyan kitma."*

[22] BT *Berakhot* 27b–28a c. SA II:75.

[23] BT *Sanhedrin* 11a–b with Rashi ad loc.

He then arose and exclaimed, "Lord of the Universe! You know full well that I have not acted thus for my honor, nor for my family's honor, but for Your honor, so that strife may not multiply in Israel!"

At that, the raging sea subsided.[24]

It appears that God believed that it was not Rabban Gamliel's pride that dictated his policies, but a sincere desire to keep the Jewish people unified in a turbulent time.

The end of the story with Rabbi Yehoshua shares this view as well. For even though he was deposed, "Rabban Gamliel was not absent from the Academy for even a single hour." He returned to the place where he had been the leader, and now sat as a simple student. While sitting in the Academy, he had yet another debate with Rabbi Yehoshua. Rabban Gamliel held that an Ammonite could not convert to Judaism based on the biblical verse of: "An Ammonite... may not enter into the assembly," while Rabbi Yehoshua held that this was no longer applicable for they are no longer the ethnic Ammonites who lived in the time of the Torah. In the spirit of the newfound freedom in the Academy, the scholars ruled according to Rabbi Yehoshua. Rabban Gamliel then realized his error: that by suppressing opinions contrary to his, he was claiming an exclusionary right to the Torah that no single individual possesses. Rabban Gamliel then apologized to Rabbi Yehoshua. He was forgiven and reinstated.[25]

---

[24] See n. 1 above.

[25] BT *Berakhot* 28a c. SA II:75.

Rabbi Hanina ben Dosa and His Wife

(First century CE)

She was accustomed to miracles.[1]

THERE ARE PEOPLE who live their lives with awareness of nothing but the Divine. They dwell in another reality where material things are insignificant, without concern for the day-to-day struggles that take up most of our energies. They are content with anything they are given and have no interest in any earthly possessions.

Then there are the people who have to live with them.

Rabbi Hanina ben Dosa, "the last miracle worker,"[2] was an outstanding, unique scholar who floated through life, fulfilling the description above. Neither money, food, nor even nature itself concerned him, for the world is full of God's presence. But while Rabbi Hanina lived his life in this idyllic fashion, his wife, whose name we do not even know, struggled to survive under the conditions that her husband's outlook caused. In the end, she succeeded.

Rabbi Hanina is remembered more for his conduct than for his halakhic teachings. There are no laws quoted in his name. Only one practice of his is mentioned as a support in a long-standing argument over whether one can begin Shabbat while it is still daytime: Rabbi Hanina would begin Shabbat at noon.[3] It is his actions that are recalled, and they are worth

---

[1] BT *Taanit* 25a c. SA II:8.

[2] Mishna *Sotah* 9:15, according to Rashi ad loc.

[3] JT *Berakhot* 5:1.

remembering. The tales told of Rabbi Hanina take place in a world full of miracles, where nature itself is subject to change with a word from his lips.

> Once on erev Shabbat he noticed that his daughter was sad.
> He said to her, "My daughter, why are you sad?"
> She replied. "My can of oil got mixed up with my can of vinegar, and I lit the Shabbat candles with vinegar."
> He said to her, "My daughter, why should this trouble you? He who has commanded that oil should burn will also command the vinegar to burn."
> The lights continued to burn throughout the entire day, and they used them for *havdala* as well.[4]

More such stories are told. When a neighbor needed longer beams to build her house, the existing beams grew at a word from Rabbi Hanina.[5] Rainfall started and stopped at his prayers.[6] A lion fled at an insult from Rabbi Hanina, though he then chased after it, apologizing profusely for having offended it.[7] When a poisonous snake was threatening the town, it was understood that Rabbi Hanina could solve the problem.

> In a certain place there was a poisonous snake that would attack people. The inhabitants told Rabbi Hanina, who said to them, "Show me its hole."
> They showed him its hole, and put his heel over it. When the snake came out and bit him, it promptly died. He put the snake on his shoulder, brought it to the Academy, and

---

[4] See n. 1 above.

[5] Ibid.

[6] BT *Taanit* 24b, c. SA ibid.

[7] Tanhuma *Va-yigash* 3 (Wassa ed.), c. SA II: 64.

taught, "See, my sons, it is not the snake that kills, rather the sin that kills."

From that occasion it was said, "Woe to the man who comes across a snake, but woe to the snake that comes across Rabbi Hanina ben Dosa."[8]

Not even food was a necessity for Rabbi Hanina, who ate only "one *kab* [four pints] of carobs from one Shabbat night to the next."[9]

The special relationship that Rabbi Hanina had with the Creator was well known, and the greatest scholars, including Rabban Gamliel and Rabbi Yohanan ben Zakkai, went to ask him to pray when their children were in danger.

> When Rabbi Hanina ben Dosa went to study Torah with Rabbi Yohanan ben Zakkai, the son of Rabbi Yohanan ben Zakkai fell ill.
>
> Rabbi Yohanan said to him, "Hanina, my son, pray for him that he may live." He put his head between his knees and prayed for him, and he lived.
>
> Rabbi Yohanan ben Zakkai said, "If ben Zakkai had put his head between his knees for the whole day, no notice would have been taken of him."
>
> His wife asked, "Is Hanina greater than you are?"
>
> He replied, "No, but he is like a servant before the king, who is free to come and go without permission, and I am like a nobleman before a king who is not often in his presence."[10]

---

8 BT *Berakhot* 33a c. SA II:63.

9 See n. 6.

10 BT *Berakhot* 34b according to Rashi ad. loc, c. SA II:65.

Setting aside the possible backhanded nature of the compliment, it was well known that Rabbi Hanina's prayers could accomplish what no one else's could. Though he himself would accredit these miraculous salvations to the merit of the individuals who were saved, strangely, when Rabbi Hanina did not pray tragedies occurred even to the most meritorious families.[11] It was said that the prayers of the Kohen Gadol on Yom Kippur were nothing when compared to those of Rabbi Hanina,[12] that for his sake "favor is shown to his [entire] generation,"[13] and "Every day a heavenly voice is heard declaring, 'The whole world draws its sustenance because of the merit of Hanina my son.'"[14]

While we do not know which profession, if any, Rabbi Hanina practiced, it is clear that it was not very lucrative. Perhaps his mind was on more transcendent things. At times this seemed to pose a problem for Rabbi Hanina, but these problems had a way of working out miraculously in the end.

> It is told that once, upon seeing the men of his town taking sacrifices up to Jerusalem, he exclaimed, "All of them bring sacrifices up to Jerusalem, and I can bring nothing! What am I to do?"
> So he went out to the waste ground of his town and found a stone, which he then chiseled, polished, and painted, and said, "I vow to take this up to Jerusalem."
> He wanted to hire some carriers, and asked them, "Will you take this stone up to Jerusalem for me?"

---

[11] BT *Yevamot* 121b and BT *Bava Kama* 50a, with comments of Pnei Yehoshua cited in Steinsaltz *Iyunim* s.v. *"Met beno be-tzama,"* c. SA II:66.

[12] See n. 6 above.

[13] BT *Hagigah* 14a.

[14] See n. 9 above.

They answered, "Pay us a hundred gold coins and we will take your stone up to Jerusalem for you."

He replied, "And where am I to get a hundred gold coins, or even fifty, to give you?"

He could not raise the money, and they went away. Immediately the Holy One, blessed be He, placed in his way five angels in the form of men. They said to him, "Master, give us five *selas* and we will take your stone up to Jerusalem, only you must help us."

He got ready to help them and immediately found himself standing in Jerusalem. He wanted to pay them but could not find them. The incident was reported in the Temple, and they said to him, "It appears, sir, that angels brought your stone up to Jerusalem."

He then gave the scholars the sum that he had agreed to pay the angels.[15]

Yet while Rabbi Hanina lived an otherworldly life replete with miracles, communing with the Divine and disregarding this world and its cares, at home his wife was struggling with the burden of having such a spiritual husband. Living in a house in which miracles are commonplace is not necessarily easy.

Rabbi Hanina ben Dosa was eating on Shabbat night when the table opened and fell on top of him.

He asked, "What is the meaning of this?"

His wife answered, "I borrowed spices from my neighbor and I didn't take *ma'aser.*"

---

[15] *Shir ha-Shirim Rabbah* 1:4, c. SA II: 61.

The spices were then put aside so that he would remember to take *ma'aser* after Shabbat, and the table rose up from upon him.[16]

She faced much greater difficulties than miraculously falling tables. As mentioned above, Rabbi Hanina's family was poor – so poor, in fact, that they were unable to afford even the ingredients to bake bread for Shabbat. His wife, embarrassed lest their neighbors discover their poverty-stricken state, would throw twigs into the oven in order to give the appearance of baking. Still, since this was Rabbi Hanina's house, the story ends in a miracle.

> She had a wicked neighbor who said, "I know that these people have nothing. What then is the meaning of all this smoke?"
>
> She went and knocked at the door. Rabbi Hanina's wife, feeling humiliated, hid in a room. A miracle occurred, and her neighbor saw the oven filled with loaves of bread and the kneading trough full of dough. The neighbor called out, "Bring your shovel, for your bread is getting charred," and she replied, "I just went to fetch it."[17]

How did Rabbi Hanina's wife respond to such a lifestyle? One tradition says that "She actually had gone to fetch the shovel because she was accustomed to miracles."[18] But can one ever truly become "accustomed to miracles"? It suited Rabbi Hanina well to live by the faith that God would ultimately intervene in any given situation. His wife, however, having had enough of their hand-to-mouth lifestyle, asked her husband to use the power

---

[16] JT *Demai* 1:3, according to Pnei Moshe ad loc.

[17] See n. 1 above.

[18] Ibid.

of his prayers to relieve them of their constant need for miraculous Divine assistance.

> Once his wife said to him, "How long shall we go on suffering so much?"
>
> "What shall we do?"
>
> "Pray that something may be given to you."
>
> He prayed, and there emerged the figure of a hand holding the leg of a golden table out to him.[19]

Though it seemed that living with a miracle worker does have its benefits, things are rarely as simple as they may appear at first. Apparently Rabbi Hanina's power of prayer was only meant to be used to help others.[20] If he wished to use this power for his own family, he would have to pay a price, as the story goes on to illustrate:

> Rabbi Hanina saw in a dream that the pious would one day eat at a three-legged golden table in the World to Come, while he would eat at a two-legged table. He asked her, "Are you content that everybody shall eat at a perfect table while we eat at an imperfect table?"

Rabbi Hanina's wife was now faced with a choice. The golden leg would alleviate their poverty, the embarrassing conditions in which they lived. No more would they have to deal with gossipy neighbors discussing how much or how little food they had. They would be able to have possessions of their own rather than merely watch over those that belonged to others. Rabbi Hanina would be able to bring a proper sacrifice to

---

[19] Ibid.

[20] Maharsha, *Hiddushei Aggadot* ad loc.

Jerusalem like everyone else instead of bringing a rock and hoping that it would be good enough. The choice of wealth over poverty must have been a tempting one to make, but Rabbi Hanina's wife had decided in favor of poverty the moment she committed herself to Rabbi Hanina.

> She replied, "What can we do? Pray that the leg should be taken away from you."
> He prayed and it was taken away.[21]

Despite her difficulties, she shared her husband's values. As challenging as her life was, she focused her attention on greater things.

Ultimately she was rewarded for her efforts, and it was Rabbi Hanina's wife who was held up as a role model for all the scholars.

> Rabbi Yohanan related: Once we were traveling aboard a ship and we saw a chest in which was set precious stones and pearls, and it was surrounded by sharks. A diver went down to bring up the chest, but a shark noticed him and was about to wrench his thigh, so he poured a bottle of vinegar upon it and the shark sank. A heavenly voice then came forward and said to us, "Why are you trying to take the chest of Rabbi Hanina ben Dosa's wife, who is to store *tekhelet* in it for the righteous in the World to Come?"[22]

---

[21] See n. 1 above.

[22] BT *Bava Batra* 74a–b.

HILLEL THE ELDER

(112 BCE–8 CE)*

Do not judge someone until you have been in his place.[1]

HILLEL THE ELDER chose to lead his life with the singular goal of becoming a scholar, though the consequence of this decision was a life of poverty. For a lesser person, this choice might have led to bitterness and the disparagement of anyone who did not choose the same lifestyle. Hillel's greatness is that he viewed everyone with respect, even people who chose wealth at the price of remaining ignorant, a priority contrary to what Hillel chose for himself. "Do not judge someone until you have been in his place" is a creed that Hillel lived by, even when he did not agree with other people's choices.

Hillel's ambitions were always clear. While his brother became wealthy in business,[2] Hillel allotted as little time to work as was necessary to pay for food and the entrance fee to the Academy, so that he could maximize the amount of time in which he could learn Torah.[3] The life he

---

* Traditions state that Hillel served as *nasi* for forty years (*Sifre* Devarim 357 c. SA II: 20), beginning one hundred years before the destruction of the Bet ha-Mikdash (BT *Shabbat* 15a). This would have been from approximately 32 BCE to 8 CE. Assuming that his term in office ended with his death, together with the tradition that he lived for 120 years (Sifre Devarim 357 c. SA II: 20), Hillel's life would have spanned from 112 BCE to 8 CE.

[1] Mishna *Avot* 2:4.

[2] BT *Sotah* 21a c. SA II:11.

[3] BT *Yoma* 35b c. SA II:12.

lived was true to his teachings, "Not all businessmen become well-learned"[4] and "Do not say: 'When I have free time I will study,' for perhaps you will never have free time."[5]

The academy charged an entrance fee during the time that Hillel was destitute. Perhaps the reason for this was to ensure that individuals who came to learn had income, that they were not studying Torah all day while their families went hungry or lived on charity.[6] Whatever the motivation, it also succeeded in keeping out sincere seekers of truth who unfortunately could not afford the fee. However, Hillel would not let that stop him.

> Every day Hillel the Elder would work and earn one coin, half of which he gave to the guard at the Academy, while he spent the other half on food for himself and his family. One day he earned nothing and the guard at the Academy would not permit him to enter. So he climbed up and sat upon the skylight in order to hear the "words of the living God" from the mouth of Shemaiah and Avtalyon [the two greatest scholars of the generation[7]]. That day was a Sabbath eve that fell upon the winter solstice, and snow fell down upon him from heaven. When dawn broke, Shemaiah said to Avtalyon, "Brother Avtalyon, every day this house is light, yet now it is dark. Perhaps it is a cloudy day?"
>
> They looked up and saw the figure of a man in the window. They went up and found him covered by three cubits [about 4.5 feet] of snow. They removed, bathed, and anointed him, and placed him opposite the fire.

---

[4] Mishna *Avot* 2:5.

[5] See n. 1 above.

[6] Steinsaltz Talmud, *Yoma* 35b, Ha-hayim s.v. "Shomer bet ha-midrash."

[7] Mishna *Avot* 1:10.

They then said, "This man deserves that the Shabbat be broken for him."[8]

Through his devotion, Hillel attained a reputation of being Shemaiah and Avtalyon's most dedicated student. After their passing, he was approached when a difficult halakhic question arose: If the day of the Pesah sacrifice falls on Shabbat, is the offering still brought? Hillel answered in the affirmative, quoting both his own logic and the tradition that he had learned from Shemaiah and Avtalyon. He was immediately appointed as the Nasi.[9] The Talmud tells us that "the halakha was hidden from the people so that Hillel would be promoted."[10]

Although Hillel was now in a position of power, he did not forget his origins. He put forward a major halakhic ruling to assist the poor in acquiring loans. According to the Torah, the right to collect payment for a loan expires after the *shemittah* (sabbatical) year. Although this law is supposed to help the destitute, preventing them from being overburdened with debt, in reality it caused people to become reluctant to lend money for fear that they would not be able to collect. The losers in this situation were the poor, who were unable to obtain the loans they needed. Hillel sought to remedy this situation by creating a legal document known as a *prozbul.*

> When he saw that people were not lending to one another, thereby transgressing what is written in the Torah, "Beware that there be not a wicked thought in your heart saying, 'The jubilee year is coming,' that causes you to look with evil at your poor brother and give him nothing," he instituted the *prozbul.*

---

[8] See n. 2.

[9] BT *Pesahim* 66a and JT *Pesahim* 6:1 c. SA II:13.

[10] JT ibid.

A *prozbul* made it possible for the lender to collect his money by inserting a special clause in the contract reading: "I declare before you, so-and-so, the judges in such-and-such a place, that regarding any debt due to me, I may be able to recover any money owing to me from so-and-so at any time I shall desire."[11]

Thus people gained confidence in the system, and the poor were able to obtain loans.

Hillel identified with the poor. A life of wealth held no appeal for him, as he taught: "More property means more anxiety... more servants mean more robbery."[12] Nevertheless, this identification did not affect the way he viewed individuals. He fully understood that people have different wants and needs, and did not invalidate the feelings of others.

> It was told of Hillel the Elder that he rented for a certain poor man who was of a good family a horse to ride upon and a servant to run before him. On one occasion he could not find a servant to run before him, so he himself ran before him for three miles.[13]

The same Hillel who taught that having servants can only cause trouble took it upon himself to give this man what he was accustomed to even though he himself considered it of little value.

Sometimes the lengths to which Hillel went to empathize with the needs of others brought him into conflict with his colleague, Shammai.

---

[11] Mishna *Sheviit* 10:3–4.

[12] Mishna *Avot* 2:7.

[13] BT *Ketubbot* 67b according to Rif ad loc., c. SA II:17.

> A certain non-Jew was passing by the Academy, when he heard the voice of a teacher reciting, "And these are the garments which they shall make: a breastplate and an ephod."
>
> The non-Jew asked, "For whom are these?"
>
> He was told, "For the Kohen Gadol."
>
> He then said to himself, "I will go and convert so that I can be appointed Kohen Gadol."
>
> So he went to Shammai and said to him, "I'll convert on condition that you appoint me Kohen Gadol."
>
> Shammai chased him away with the measuring stick that was in his hand.

Shammai's response to the prospective convert is predictable. If someone wants to convert for material gain, it is certainly logical to reject him as insincere (putting aside the other problem, that according to halakha a convert cannot become a Kohen – a status that is inherited from the father – much less the Kohen Gadol). What is surprising is the fact that Hillel did convert him.

Hillel, who shunned wealth for himself due to his belief that it interferes with one's spiritual development, did not take it upon himself to judge the prospective convert's motives. Instead, he accommodated him on his own terms. True to his teachings, he did not believe in judging people, but rather in accepting them as they were.

The convert eventually gave up his aspirations to become the Kohen Gadol and uttered a phrase to Hillel that any Jew may honestly say of this great leader:

"Humble Hillel, may you be blessed for bringing me under the Divine Presence."[14]

---

[14] BT *Shabbat* 31 c. SA II:16.

RABBI MEIR

(Second century CE)

An anonymous teaching represents the view of Rabbi Meir. [1]

RABBI MEIR'S[2] LIFE was filled with persecution, exile, and attempts on his life. The Romans, offended by his conduct, tried to have him killed. The religious establishment wanted him banned from public life. Even God Himself, displeased with his beliefs, wished to have his name erased from history. Still, Rabbi Meir is remembered for leaving an immeasurable impact on halakha and therefore on Jewish existence as a whole.

One needs only to look at the fate of his teachers to get a sense of the time and place in which Rabbi Meir lived. His primary teacher was Rabbi Akiva, who was the first rabbi to ordain him (though this ordination was not ultimately accepted due to Rabbi Meir's youth at the time).[3] Rabbi Akiva was brutally murdered by the Roman occupying government in a public spectacle for the crime of teaching Torah in public.[4] His second teacher, Rabbi Yehuda ben Bava, who ordained him, was also killed by the Romans. This time, Rabbi Meir was directly involved in the tragedy.

---

[1] According to BT *Eruvin* 13b (c. SA II:189), the name Meir was just a nickname because he "enlightened" (*meir*) the eyes of the scholars in halakha. His birth name was either Nehorai or, more likely, Maissa (see *Dikdukei Sofrim* ad loc.).

[2] BT *Sanhedrin* 86a.

[3] BT *Sanhedrin* 14a, Rashi ad loc.

[4] BT *Berakhot* 61a, c. SA II:177. See chapter on Rabbi Akiva above.

Once the wicked government decreed that whoever granted or received ordination should be put to death, the city in which the ordination took place demolished, and the boundaries where it had been performed uprooted. What did Rabbi Yehudah ben Bava do? He went between two great mountains that were between two large cities, between the boundaries of the cities of Usha and Shefaram, and ordained scholars. As soon as their enemies discovered them, Rabbi Yehuda ben Bava urged them, "My children, flee!"

They responded, "What will become of you, Rabbi?"

He replied, "I will lie before them like a stone that no one is interested in overturning."

It was said that the enemy did not stir from the spot until they had driven three hundred iron spearheads into his body, making his body like a sieve.[5]

His third teacher had the most tragic fate of all. For while Rabbis Akiva and Yehuda ben Bava are forever remembered as heroes, Rabbi Meir's third teacher, Elisha ben Avuyah, is remembered as an apostate.[6] Even worse, he was a traitor who taught the Romans exactly what actions would force the Jews to violate the greatest number of *halakhot*.[7] Much to the disapproval of his colleagues, Rabbi Meir continued to learn from Elisha, who was the only one of his teachers to survive, even after his apostasy.[8] Convinced that Elisha had repented before he died,[9] Rabbi Meir vowed to

---

[5] BT *Sanhedrin* 14a.

[6] BT *Hagigah* 15a–b, c. SA II:191. See chapter on Elisha ben Avuyah above.

[7] JT *Hagigah* 2:1.

[8] BT *Hagigah,* ibid.; JT *Hagigah,* ibid.; *Ruth Rabbah* 6:2, *Kohelet Rabbah* 7:16 c. SA ibid.

[9] JT *Hagigah* ibid.; *Ruth Rabbah* ibid.; *Kohelet Rabbah* ibid. c. SA ibid.

intercede on his teacher's behalf after his own death to obtain a share in the afterlife for Elisha.[10]

The Roman persecutors eventually focused their attention on Meir as well. His father-in-law, Rabbi Hanina ben Teradion, was tortured to death for teaching Torah publicly, while his daughter was placed in a brothel. Upon the request of his wife Beruriah, a scholar in her own right, he went to rescue his sister-in-law. Disguised as a guard, he went prepared with bribes and removed her successfully from the brothel. However, his act was soon discovered by the Roman authorities.

> They engraved a picture of Rabbi Meir on the gates of Rome and proclaimed that anyone seeing a person resembling it should bring him there. One day some Romans saw him and ran after him, so he ran away from them and entered a house of prostitution. Others say he happened just then to see food cooked by non-Jews, so he dipped one finger in it and then sucked the other [giving the appearance that he ate non-kosher food]. Others again say that Eliyahu ha-Navi appeared to the soldiers as a harlot and embraced Rabbi Meir.
>
> Some say: God forbid that Rabbi Meir would act in such a way. Instead, he fled to Babylon.[11]

The Romans' attempt to assassinate Rabbi Meir did not succeed. He eventually returned safely to Israel, where he played a major role in the re-establishment of the High Court, which at the time was located in the town of Usha.[12]

---

[10] BT *Hagigah,* ibid.; JT *Hagigah* ibid.; *Kohelet Rabbah* ibid. c. SA ibid.

[11] BT *Avodah Zarah* 18a–b, c. SA II:180, 210.

[12] *Shir ha-Shirim Rabbah* 2:18

But Rabbi Meir still faced opposition from a far greater adversary. It seems that God, displeased with Rabbi Meir's loyalty to Elisha ben Avuyah, wished for Rabbi Meir's name to be erased from the history of halakha. Eventually, even He was convinced otherwise.

> Rabbah ben Shila once met Eliyahu ha-Navi.
>
> Rabbah asked him, "What is the Holy One, blessed be He, doing?"
>
> He answered, "He utters traditions in the name of all the rabbis except for Rabbi Meir."
>
> Rabbah asked him, "Why?"
>
> "Because he learned from Aher [Elisha ben Auyah]."
>
> Rabbah replied to him, "But why not? Rabbi Meir found a pomegranate. He ate the fruit within it and threw away the rind."
>
> He answered, "Now God says: 'Meir, my son, says.'"[13]

Although the Roman Empire and God Himself did not succeed in wiping out Rabbi Meir's name, internal Jewish politics almost did. Once the High Court was re-established, the three greatest sages were given titles. Rabbi Meir was called Hakham, Rabbi Natan was Head of the Court, and Rabbi Shimon, the son of Rabbi Gamliel of Yavneh, was Nasi. All three positions were accorded equal respect, with everyone rising to their feet in the presence of any of them. However, Rabbi Shimon disapproved, since he felt that his office deserved more respect than the other two. One day, when Rabbis Natan and Meir were not present, Rabbi Shimon passed a new law.

> When the Nasi enters, all the people rise and do not resume their seats until he asks them to sit. When the Head of the

---

[13] BT *Hagigah* 15b c. SA 193.

Court enters, one row rises on one side and another row on the other and remain standing until he has sat down in his place. When the Hakham enters, every one whom he passes rises and sits down as soon as he passed until he sits down in his place.

Thus the first shot was fired in what would become a battle pitting Rabbi Meir's followers against the esteemed House of Gamliel.

Rabbis Natan and Meir hatched a plan to expose Rabbi Shimon's weaknesses publicly, hoping that this would force him to resign from his post.

When they came on the following day and saw that the people did not rise for them as usual, they inquired as to what had happened. Upon being told that R. Shimon ben Gamliel had proclaimed the new law, Rabbi Meir said to Rabbi Nathan, "I am the Hakham and you are the Head of the Court. Let us retaliate.... Let us ask him to teach the tractate of Ukzin, which he doesn't know. When he is unable to teach it... we will depose him, and I shall become Head of the Court and you will become the Nasi."

Fortunately for Rabbi Shimon, the plot was discovered by Rabbi Yaakov ben Korshai, who thwarted it in the interests of preventing a public spectacle.

Rabbi Yaakov ben Korshai heard this conversation and said, 'The matter might, God forbid, lead to Rabbi Shimon's disgrace.'
So he sat down behind Rabbi Shimon's study and recited the tractate of Ukzin, repeating it over and over.

Rabbi Shimon said, "What could this mean? Could something be happening at the Academy?" So he concentrated his attention to Rabbi Yaakov's recital and familiarized himself with it. On the following day when they said to him, "Will the Master teach Ukzin?", he taught it.

This did not avert the conflict, but rather escalated it.

After Rabbi Shimon had finished he said to Rabbis Natan and Meir, "Had I not familiarized myself with it, you would have disgraced me!"
He gave the order and they were removed from the academy.[14]

Thus Rabbi Meir, who endured so much for the sake of the Torah and his people, was now thrown out of the academy. According to one source there was even an attempt to excommunicate him. Fortunately, it failed.[15] Still, as little as Rabbi Shimon wanted him around, he had to admit that he needed him.

Rabbis Natan and Meir would write down questions on slips of paper and throw them into the academy. Those which Rabbi Shimon could answer were disposed of, and for those that he could not solve, Rabbis Natan and Meir wrote down the answers and threw them in.
Rabbi Yose then said to the scholars in the academy. "The Torah is outside and we are inside!"
Rabbi Shimon then announced, "We shall readmit them."

[14] BT *Horayot* 13b c. SA II:277, JT *Bikkurim* 3:3.

[15] JT *Moed Katan* 3:1.

There was, however, one condition:

> "The following penalty shall be imposed upon them: that no statements shall be reported in their names."

Eventually Rabbi Natan apologized, but Rabbi Meir refused. Thus a political dispute succeeded in accomplishing what others had failed to do: erasing Rabbi Meir from history.[16]

There is a postscript, however. A man of Rabbi Meir's status cannot remain hidden for long, and the House of Gamliel admitted that his learning was more important than his politics.

> Rabbi Yehuda the son of Rabbi Shimon taught his son, Rabbi Shimon: "Others say…" His son asked him, "Who are those whose waters we drink but whose names we do not mention?"
> Rabbi Yehuda answered him, "These are men who wished to uproot your dignity and the dignity of your father's house."
> His son said to him, "Their love, hatred, and envy have already perished."
> Rabbi Yehuda said to him, "The enemy has disappeared, but their swords are forever."
> His son responded, "This phrase applies only if their actions were successful, which in this case they were not."
> Rabbi Yehuda then repeated the lesson, adding: "It was said in the name of Rabbi Meir."[17]

---

[16] See note 14 above.

[17] BT *Horayot* 13b–14a, c. SA II:216.

RAV PAPA
(300–375 CE)[1]

I was once suspected of something of which I was innocent.[2]

RAV PAPA LIVED in two worlds. On the one hand, he was a respected scholar known for his learning and humility. On the other, he was immersed in the material world, an ambitious businessman who enjoyed his success. There is a line between simply making use of material bounty and being consumed by it, and some thought that Rav Papa crossed that line.

A successful businessman, Rav Papa took pleasure in the results of his hard work. Of him it was said that he "received what he earned in this world."[3] He enjoyed his food and was known to eat four times the amount that other scholars ate. Rav Papa would not give halakhic rulings on Shabbat since he drank too much to be clearheaded, and claimed that "Whoever can drink beer but drinks wine instead violates the commandment 'Do not waste.'"[4] A story is told about how a fellow scholar attempted to engage in a legal jousting match with Rav Papa over dinner. In response, Rav Papa

---

[1] *Sefer ha-Eshkol,* Hilkhot Sefer Torah 60b cites the Hai Gaon's comment that the many "sons of Papa" listed in the *Hadran* prayer recited upon completing a tractate lived at various times and therefore cannot all be the children of our Rav Papa.

[2] BT *Shabbat* 118b and *Moed Katan* 18b c. SA II:724.

[3] BT *Horayot* 10b c. SA II:721.

[4] BT *Shabbat* 140b c. SA II:723.

uttered a simple prayer: "May it be His will that the rest of this ox be eaten in peace."[5]

These luxuries came as a result of his success in business, which Rav Papa mainly attributed to luck by entering the right industry (brewing beer)[6] and marrying into the right family (a kohen's daughter).[7] Still, a survey of his business dealings shows that he took his finances seriously and was not always easy to deal with.

> Rav Papa and Rav Huna bought some sesame on the bank of a canal. They hired some boatmen who guaranteed the delivery, and in the event of an accident to bring it across. After a time the canal was stopped up.
>
> They said to the boatmen, "Hire donkeys and deliver the goods to us, since you have given us a guarantee in the event of an accident."
>
> The boatmen appealed to Raba, who told them, "These old men even want to strip these boatmen of their clothes! This is a rare situation for which they are not liable."[8]

Even Rav Papa's dealings with his prospective in-laws were imposing. Judah bar Meremar did not want to accompany him to the negotiations with Abbah of Sura over the dowry for his daughter's marriage to Rav Papa's son, fearing that it would look like he was siding with Rav Papa in the negotiations. His fears were well founded, since at the end the negotiations Abbah exclaimed "I have nothing left for myself!"[9] Still, Rav

---

[5] BT *Niddah* 33b c. SA II:728.

[6] BT *Pesahim* 113a c. SA II:722.

[7] BT *Pesahim* 49a c. SA ibid.

[8] BT *Gittin* 73a according to Rashi ad loc. c. SA II:727.

[9] BT *Ketubbot* 52b–53a c. SA II:730.

Papa had a reputation for letting the welfare of others dictate his negotiations even if this meant that he would lose money in the process.

> If a man sold a plot of land to obtain money for a specific purpose but on the conclusion of the sale he no longer needs the money for that purpose, can he renege on the sale or not?
>
> Come and hear: Once someone sold a plot of land to Rav Papa because he needed money to buy some oxen. By the time the deal was completed the man was no longer in need of the money and regretted selling the land. Rav Papa returned the land to him. However, this does not prove that this is the law, for Rav Papa would act beyond the letter of the law.[10]

Food and business were not Rav Papa's only interests. The accounts in the Talmud show him to be a learned and sensitive man who desperately avoided offending others and took to heart what others said about him. He took great care to honor scholars, going out of his way to pay his respects.[11] "I am praised," he said, "because I have never excommunicated a scholar."[12] He did his best to act generously even toward those who disagreed with him, treating with the greatest respect. When he felt that he had spoken unkindly of his colleagues, he would fast[13] even though fasting was very difficult for him.[14] He even treated those who did not respect him, such as the three former disciples of Rabbah who came to him to study, with honor and love.

---

[10] BT *Ketubbot* 97a according to Steinsaltz ad loc.

[11] Ibid.

[12] BT *Moed Katan* 17a.

[13] BT *Sanhedrin* 100a.

[14] BT *Taanit* 24b c. SA II:734.

Apparently, they were unimpressed with Rav Papa's knowledge and spent the lessons snickering at their new teacher. As they left him to find another teacher, he blessed them, saying, "May the rabbis go in peace."[15] Although Rav Papa was hurt by their behavior, he forgave them and wished them well.

Given Rav Papa's business and gastronomic interests, accusations regarding his religious sincerity and even his halakhic observance were bound to arise. Upon hearing Rabbi Yose's statement of "May my portion be with those who, though innocent, are under suspicion," Rav Papa remarked, "I was suspected of something of which I was innocent."[16] What was this accusation of which Rav Papa spoke? One talmudic tradition hints that the accusation was baseless and does not even mention it.[17] However, the commentators are not so quick to dismiss it. Some[18] point to a strange story, told to teach the moral lesson behind the dictum, "Do not sit on the couch of an Aramean woman."

> There was an Aramean woman who owed Rav Papa money, and he would visit her house daily to collect it from her. One day she strangled her son and put the corpse under the bed. When Rav Papa came in she said to him, "Sit while I bring you your money," and he did so. When she returned she said "You killed my son!" He then fled the country.[19]

That is certainly possible, though in an earlier account of the story, Rav Papa discovers the corpse before sitting down, thus avoiding any accusation.[20] Another possibility[21] relates an accusation by Rabbis Samma[22]

---

[15] BT Taanit 9a–b.

[16] See n. 2.

[17] BT *Moed Katan* 18b.

[18] The Maharshal on *Bava Batra* 10a c. Artscroll Tractate *Shabbat* 118b (3).

[19] Rashi, *Pesahim* 112b c. SA 733.

[20] BT *Berakhot* 8b c. SA ibid.

and Hiyya bar Rav[23] that he was overly frugal in giving charity. Although this may be possible, another accusation was much worse: it inferred that his commitment to Torah was only secondary to his other interests.

We know that Rav Papa was intense in his business dealings. We know that some people felt he crossed the line. But an accusation circulated among his colleagues that went beyond mere displeasure at his methods. He was accused of doing no less than violating the biblical prohibition of usury.

As we know, Rav Papa was a brewer. Like any businessman, he sold on credit. Though the halakha states that one may not overcharge for the purchase price while selling on credit, Rav Papa did so. His rationale was that if he wanted to, he could refrain from selling his beer, wait until prices rose, and sell it then. Thus he was not really benefiting by selling on credit. He was only helping the buyer.

However, Rav Papa's clarification of this practice did not appease all of his colleagues.

> Rav Sheshet replied, "Why do you only think of your side of the deal? Think about the buyer. If he had the money, he would purchase at the current price, but since he does not, he must buy it at the higher future price."[24]

As far as we know, Rav Papa did not change his policy and Rav Sheshet did not withdraw his accusation. In this case the Talmud, as understood by the commentators, follows Rav Sheshet's opinion that Rav Papa's practice was indeed illegal.[25]

---

[21] *Megadim Hadashim,* c. Artscroll, ibid.

[22] BT *Bava Batra* 9a c. SA II:731.

[23] BT *Bava Batra* 10a c. SA II:732.

[24] BT *Bava Metzia* 65a.

[25] Bet Yosef, *Yoreh Deah* 173.

If that is the case, how do we view this complex character? If in an encounter between the physical and the spiritual he succumbed to the former, can he still be revered as a great teacher? Indeed, some scholars mocked Rav Papa's piety as a sham.

> Rav Papa ordained a fast but no rain fell. He began to feel faint, so he ate a bowlful of grits and prayed more, but still no rain fell. Rabbi Nahman ben Ushpazarti then said to him, "Perhaps if you were to eat another bowlful of grits, rain would fall."

Perhaps our view of Rav Papa should be similar to that of Rabbi Nahman: that regardless of his facade as a declarer of fasts, the true Rav Papa is the man who eats on a fast day.

However, we know that it is not the case. A person's interests in the material aspects of the world do not necessarily conflict with spiritual pursuits. Rav Papa may have not been built for fasting, but his eating was a purer act than the fasts of many others. At the end of this story, God Himself demonstrates that regardless of his physical appetites, Rav Papa's piety is sincere.

"Rav Papa felt humiliated and faint, and rain fell."[26]

---

[26] See n. 14 above, Steinsaltz "lashon" s.v. Pinka (renders it as large bowl against Rashi's spoonful).

RAVA AND ABAYE

(Abaye: 278–338 CE; Rava: d. 352 CE)

In our dreams we both read the verse, "All the peoples of the earth will see that you are called by the name of the Lord."[1]

RABBI SHMUEL BEN NAHMANI said in the name of Rabbi Yonatan, "A man is shown in a dream only what is suggested by his own thoughts…." Rava said, "The proof of this is that no one was ever shown in a dream a date palm of made of gold or an elephant going through the eye of a needle."[2]

If the above is true (and psychologists since Freud have argued that it is), what can we make of two scholars who dreamed exactly the same dreams? This is one issue that we find when we encounter Abaye[3] and Rava,[4] two scholars who play a primary role in the Babylonian Talmud. More accurately, their disagreements play a primary role, so much so that Talmudic discussion is often simply called "the arguments of Abaye and Rava."[5]

The relationship between Abaye and Rava began when they were very young. Abaye, whose "father died at his conception and mother died at

---

[1] BT *Berakhot* 56a c. SA II:715.

[2] BT *Berakhot* 55b–56a.

[3] Also called Nahmani.

[4] His birth name was Abba. Rava is a merging of "Rav Abba."

[5] Rambam, Hilkhot Yesodei ha-Torah 4:13, based on BT *Sukkah* 28a.

his birth,"[6] was raised by his uncle Rabbah,[7] a great scholar who taught his adopted charge. Rava also "sat before Rabbah," apparently learning from the great scholar during his youth. Even in childhood, Abaye and Rava could not answer a question in the same way even when they seemed to be saying the very same thing.

> As children, Abaye and Rava were once sitting before Rabbah.
>
> Rabbah asked them, "To whom do we say blessings?"
>
> They answered, "To God."
>
> "And where is God?"
>
> Rava pointed to the ceiling and Abaye went outside and pointed to the sky.[8]

As they grew older, the feeling of competition clearly remained between them. When one claimed that "In Tiberias I am considered as sharp as Ben Azzai," the other followed suit with the same statement.[9]

At times, the desire of one of them to distinguish himself from the other took a form of one-upmanship, such as discussing the difficulty in remaining focused while studying. When Abaye stated, "If my foster mother had merely asked me to bring her a dish, I would not have been able to study," Rava responded, "Even if a louse bit me I would not have been able to study"[10] (even with lice being more common in those days).

---

[6] BT *Kiddushin* 31b c. SA II:669.

[7] His real name was Rav Abba as well. Sherira Gaon tells us that Rabbah was Abaye's paternal uncle and that Abaye was named Nahmani for his own grandfather, who was also Rabbah's father.

[8] BT *Berakhot* 48a c. SA II:671.

[9] BT *Kiddushin* 20a c. SA II:673 and BT *Eruvin* 29a c. SA II:694.

[10] BT *Eruvin* 65a c. SA II:695.

Even the occasion of Rav Ada bar Ahava's sudden death became a topic of debate between the two. Abaye claimed that the lack of respect that Rav Ada showed him had led to the former's demise, while Rava countered, "He was punished on my account, for when he went to the butcher shop he would say, 'Serve me before the servant of Rava because I am superior to him.'"[11]

Their disagreements were not always harmless. At one point, Rava's envy of his childhood friend threw him into depression. Although he graciously ceded to Abaye the position of Head of the Academy, which had been held previously by Rava's teacher Rav Yoseph, when Abaye defeated him in an intellectual jousting match,[12] other things were more difficult for him to accept.

> Abaye received greetings from the Heavenly Academy every Erev Shabbat, while Rava received them every Erev Yom Kippur.... Rava was dejected because of the special honor shown to Abaye.[13]

Although Abaye was Head of the Academy, he, too, had trouble escaping from Rava's shadow. Though Rava had ceded the position, some clearly thought that he deserved it.

> Rabbi Ada bar Ahava used to say to the students in Abaye's academy, "Instead of gnawing bones in Abaye's school, why don't you eat good meat in Rava's?"[14]

---

[11] BT *Bava Batra* 22a c. SA II:707.

[12] BT *Horayot* 14a according to Beit Shmuel cited in Steinsaltz ad loc; c. SA II:672.

[13] BT *Taanit* 21b–22a c. SA II:677.

[14] See n. 11 above.

It appears that from their childhood as pupils to their adulthood as well-respected scholars, Abaye and Rava lived their lives in the shadow of one another. Their arguments, one-upmanship, and jealousies can only be understood if we understand why each one had such a profound effect on the other's life. What is the source of this influence?

It lies in their similarities. These two men had so much in common that they looked for ways in which to distinguish themselves. Their similarity can be seen through a glimpse into the clearest vantage points into a person's soul, his dreams. As the Talmud states (and Rava agreed), "A man is shown in a dream only what is suggested by his own thoughts." On the occasions when Abaye and Rava went to have their dreams interpreted, it became clear how much the two scholars' very thoughts had in common. Over time,[15] they both dreamed that

> We both read the verse "Your ox will be slain before your eyes but you will not eat it, your donkey will be violently taken away from right in front of you and will not be returned, your sheep will be given to your enemies and you will not rescue them," and the verse "You will father sons and daughters but you will not enjoy them since they will go into captivity," and the verse "Your sons and daughters will be given to another people while your eyes gaze with longing for them all day long but there will be no strength in your hand," and the verse "Go on your way, eat your bread with joy and drink your wine with a happy heart, for God has accepted your work," and the verse "You will bring a great deal of seed into the field but will gather little in, for the locusts will eat it," and the verse "You will have olive trees throughout your land but you will not anoint yourself

---

[15] Ya'avetz, cited in Steinsaltz Talmud, *Berakhot* 56a.

with the oil since your olive trees will drop their fruit," and the verse "All the peoples of the earth will see that you are called by the name of the Lord and will fear you."

In our dreams, we both saw a head of lettuce on the mouth of a jar, some meat on the mouth of a jar, a cask hanging on a palm tree, a cask fall into a pit, and a young donkey standing by our pillow and braying.[16]

As the Talmud tells us, the meaning of these dreams is a matter of interpretation. What is relevant is that here are two men who dreamed the same dream on at least twelve different occasions. For all the disputes that they had, these two men were remarkably similar. This common ground is what allowed them to take issue with each other on so many occasions even as they jointly held the mantle of leadership of their time.

Abaye and Rava were not conflicting personalities. Rather, they were like two banks of a river separated by a geological fault. At root, these two scholars were of a single essence. As the Talmud says:

Upon the deaths of Abaye and Rava, the rocks of the Tigris kissed each other.[17]

---

[16] See n. 1 above.

[17] BT *Moed Katan* 25b c. SA 720.

RESH LAKISH

(Third century CE)

Anyone who raises his hand in a violent manner toward his friend, even if he does not strike him, is called a rasha *[an evildoer]*.[1]

RABBI SHIMON BEN LAKISH, or Resh Lakish as he is more commonly known, was known as a great scholar with impeccable moral standing. Scholars would gather to learn from him the teachings of his teacher and colleague, Rabbi Yohanan ben ha-Nappah,[2] and his reputation for honesty was so great that "Anyone who spoke with Resh Lakish in the marketplace could get a loan without witnesses."[3] However, behind this ideal picture lay a troubled past that eventually caught up with him and led to his ruin.

Some of Resh Lakish's behavior seems unusual for a scholar. For example, when Rav Imi was kidnapped and presumed dead, Resh Lakish volunteered to undertake, and successfully carried out, a one-man rescue mission.[4] Later, upon hearing that Rabbi Yohanan had been robbed, Resh Lakish went out and tracked down the thieves.[5] Although such acts are unusual for one who preached the value of constant Torah study,[6] Resh

---

[1] BT *Sanhedrin* 58b c. SA II:45.

[2] BT *Bava Kama* 117a, Rashi ad loc. s.v. *Mesayaim* c. SA II:422.

[3] BT *Yoma* 9b c. SA II:423.

[4] JT *Terumot* 8:10 c. SA II:434.

[5] Ibid.

[6] BT *Gittin* 57b.

Lakish's background was radically different from that of a typical yeshiva student.

We know nothing about his childhood. In one talmudic statement, he implies that he learned Torah "from his fathers," but the Talmud quickly qualifies that by saying, "Others say, 'I learned it from Rabbi Yehuda's fathers.'"[7] All we know for certain is that before he became a great scholar, his life had been one long tale of violence. After selling himself as a gladiator, he did not fight in the stadium but rather killed his owners, bludgeoning them to death with a stone and then fleeing.[8] On the run, he encountered Rabbi Yohanan, most probably with the intention of robbing him.[9] Rabbi Yohanan, impressed by his great strength, chided him, saying, "Your strength should be devoted to Torah." To which Resh Lakish, equally impressed by Rabbi Yohanan's good looks, replied, "Your beauty should be devoted to women." So they struck a deal: Resh Lakish would repent and join the world of the scholars, and in return would be given the privilege of marrying Rabbi Yohanan's beautiful sister.[10] The deal was a success on both sides. Resh Lakish thrived in the Academy, and a nephew was born to Rabbi Yohanan.

From that point on, Resh Lakish threw his whole being into Torah study. His physical strength decreased as his focus shifted to spiritual matters.[11] "One who saw Resh Lakish studying would think he was uprooting mountains and grinding them one against the other."[12] He would

---

[7] BT *Shabbat* 119a.

[8] BT *Gittin* 47a c. SA II:419.

[9] BT *Bava Metzia* 84a, Rashi ad loc. s.v. *Hazyah* c. SA II:420.

[10] BT ibid c. SA ibid.

[11] Ibid.

[12] BT *Sanhedrin* 24a c. SA II:424.

wander aimlessly, unaware of where he was headed, as he meditated on the Torah.[13]

As his learning grew, so did his confidence. "Unlike others, I can both connect different passages and penetrate their meaning."[14] When he believed he was right, he would argue with anyone, even his master Rabbi Yohanan or the Patriarch himself, Rabbi Yehuda ha-Nasi.[15] Although he criticized those whom he felt were lax in keeping the law, whether for their weak observance of sabbatical year[16] or, in the case of the Babylonian scholars, for not moving to Israel,[17] he was very harsh with those who spoke negatively about the Jews of Israel. On one occasion he washed Rabbi Abbahu's mouth out with dirt for having done so.[18]

Nevertheless, his violent past always lurked in the background. He tried to redeem his past actions by using the skills that he acquired to help others, as in the cases of the kidnapping of Rav Imi and the theft of Rabbi Yohanan's money. He renounced his old ways, saying, "A man should always incite his good inclination against his evil inclination"[19] and "Every day a man's evil inclination threatens to master him and seeks to kill him."[20] "If a scholar becomes angry, his wisdom departs from him; if a prophet, his prophecy departs from him."[21] Finally, in one of his most radical statements against violence, he tried to wipe out all traces of his previous life, saying:

---

[13] JT *Berakhot* 5:1 c. SA II:425.

[14] *Shir ha-Shirim Rabbah* 1:10 c. SA II:427.

[15] JT *Sanhedrin* 2:1.

[16] BT *Sanhedrin* 26a, c. SA II:430.

[17] BT *Yoma* 9b.

[18] *Shir ha-Shirim Rabbah* 1:6 c. SA II:433.

[19] BT *Berakhot* 5a.

[20] BT *Sukkah* 52b.

[21] BT *Pesahim* 66b.

Anyone who raises his hand in a violent manner toward his friend, even if he does not strike him, is called an evildoer.

But in the end, he could not hide his past any longer. Sadly, the man who blew his cover, who revealed what he had tried to keep hidden for so long, was none other than his teacher, friend, and brother-in-law, Rabbi Yohanan himself.

From the time of the fateful meeting between Rav Yohanan and Resh Lakish, their relationship progressed from that of teacher and student to that of close friends and colleagues. At a glance, these two men appeared to have very little in common. While Resh Lakish came from a criminal background, Rabbi Yohanan came from a scholarly family and had been immersed in Torah from his childhood.[22] Rabbi Yohanan's connection to Torah was so strong that Rabbi Yehuda applied to him the verse "[God said:] 'Even before I formed you in the womb, I knew you.'"[23] Yet it was the great differences between Resh Lakish and Rabbi Yohanan that made their relationship so strong. Rabbi Yohanan said that when he raised a point, "Ben Lakish would raise twenty-four objections, thereby starting a debate that led to a fuller understanding of the tradition."[24] He came to respect Resh Lakish's objections so much that when he was told that Resh Lakish disagreed with his ruling, he would respond, "What can I do when one of equal authority disagrees with me?"[25] It was during one of these disagreements that Rabbi Yohanan let slip a statement that broke Resh Lakish's spirit and ultimately led to both of their deaths.

As is often the case, the discussion began simply. It revolved around the question of at what point during a weapon's manufacture it is considered

---

[22] TJ *Ma'aserot* 1:2 c. SA II:400.

[23] BT *Yoma* 82b c. SA II:398.

[24] BT *Bava Metzia* 84a c. SA II:436.

[25] BT *Ketubbot* 54b, 84b.

to be completed, since before that point it would not be susceptible to ritual impurity. Rabbi Yohanan said, "After it has been tempered in a furnace." As usual, Resh Lakish disagreed, ruling, "Only after it has been quenched in water." To which Rabbi Yohanan remarked, "So the robber is an expert in his trade."[26]

Why did Rabbi Yohanan say such a thing? Was it a snide remark that he had held back for years, a sharp reminder that no matter how well respected Resh Lakish might become, he, Rabbi Yohanan, would always know his true background? Or could it have been a good-natured jab at an old and dear friend, conceding that Resh Lakish is correct in this halakha since he knows better from personal experience? We will never know.

We know only that unfortunately, Resh Lakish took this statement in the worst possible way, telling Rabbi Yohanan not to think that he had done him any favors, since "before, I was called a master, and now I am called a master." Rabbi Yohanan, seeing this as a slight to all that he had done for him, answered that Resh Lakish owed him everything, saying, "I brought you under the Divine Presence." The two companions parted ways, but each one suffered terribly over the loss of the friendship.

Resh Lakish fell ill, while Rabbi Yohanan regretted what he had said. But as is too often the case, neither one would forgive the other. Fearing the worst – that Resh Lakish would die of a broken heart – his wife went to plead with her brother for a reconciliation, but her efforts availed nothing. Resh Lakish died a broken man.[27] Rabbi Yohanan's sister severed all ties between her brother and her children,[28] and Rabbi Yohanan, consumed with remorse and longing for his old comrade, went insane and died.[29]

---

[26] See n. 24 above.

[27] Ibid.

[28] BT *Ta'anit* 9a c. SA II:437.

[29] See n. 24 above.

As with many tragedies, it is difficult to hold only one side responsible. Perhaps Resh Lakish should have realized that he would never be able to erase his past completely and learn how to accept it. For his part, Rabbi Yohanan could have shown more sensitivity to Resh Lakish and been more careful with his words. Still, if one looks in the Talmud today, there is hardly a page where Rabbi Yohanan and Resh Lakish do not appear side by side, disagreeing respectfully on almost every issue under discussion. Their names do not call to mind the tension of their final days, but rather the hundreds of discussions between them that shaped the future of Jewish life. The image of Rabbi Yohanan and Resh Lakish is that of ideal study partners whom generations of future students would remember as the "two renowned authorities."[30]

---

[30] JT *Berakhot* 8:7.

SHMUEL

(end of second to middle of third century)

Had I been there, I would have given a better proof than them all.[1]

SHMUEL WAS BORN in the wrong place in history. From childhood, he felt that he had a destiny to fulfill, and he amassed the knowledge and self-confidence that were necessary to leave his mark on Jewish tradition. However, by the time he grew to be a scholar, the era was already at an end, and its great work, the Mishna, was already completed.[2] Nevertheless, this did not stop Shmuel from throwing himself into debates that preceded that work and taking issue with the revered scholars of previous generations. Ultimately, Shmuel is remembered as the man who fought with giants and won.

Shmuel's first confrontation with a senior authority occurred when he was a child.

> Shmuel's father once saw his son crying and asked him, "Why are you crying?"
>
> "Because my teacher beat me," Shmuel replied.
>
> "Why did he beat you?"
>
> "He said to me 'You fed my son and you did not wash your hands first.'"
>
> "So why didn't you wash?"

---

[1] BT *Yoma* 85b, *Megillah* 7a, *Hagigah* 10a.

[2] The assumption that Shmuel was a child at the time of the Mishna's compilation stems from the fact that as a child, Shmuel knew Levi ben Sisi (see n. 4 below), who was a colleague of Rabbi Yehudah ha-Nasi (BT *Berakhot* 49a, *Shabbat* 107b, *Zevahim* 30b, *Menahot* 80b), who compiled the Mishna.

"He was the one who was eating, so why should I wash?"

Fortunately for Shmuel, his father was an understanding man who would not subject his son to the ignorance of others, regardless of their superior social position.

> Shmuel's father said, "It is bad enough that your teacher is ignorant, but must he also beat you?!"[3]

The self-confidence that his father instilled in him stayed with him even after his father's untimely death. Upon hearing that his father had been accused posthumously of taking money that orphans deposited with him, Shmuel investigated the case. The obvious problem – that his father was no longer alive – did not bother him, since he went to the cemetery to talk with spirits who would be the most likely to know where his father was. Unfortunately, there was some confusion because his father's name was Abba the son of Abba, which also means "a father the son of a father."

> When he went to find his father at the cemetery, he told the dead, "I am looking for Abba."
> They replied, "There are many Abbas [fathers] here."
> "I want Abba the son of Abba."
> They replied, "There are also several people called Abba the son of Abba here."

Eventually he cleared up the confusion by asking for "Abba the son of Abba, the father of Shmuel." He was then referred to the obvious location for a deceased scholar, the Heavenly Academy. Upon his arrival, he

---

[3] BT *Hullin* 107b c. SA II:551.

was distressed to see that Levi,[4] a friend of his father's,[5] had been denied entry. When he found his father, they began to talk.

> When Shmuel saw that his father was crying and laughing, he asked him, "Why are you crying?"
> He replied, "Because you are coming here soon."
> "So why are you laughing?"
> "Because you are highly esteemed in this world."
> Shmuel then said, "If I am esteemed, then let them take Levi in," and they took Levi in.[6]

We can gain two insights from this story. The first is that Shmuel always knew that he was destined for greatness. We later hear that Shmuel saw in the "Book of Adam" that he would be a scholar.[7] The second is that he had no problem stating what he felt was right.

Shmuel kept his self-assurance as he grew to be a religious leader (although he was never officially ordained as a rabbi,[8] since in those momentous times one did not need a mere title to be a halakhic authority). Upon observing the exploitation that merchants practiced around holiday times, Shmuel used his authority to lower prices. He threatened the myrtle merchants that if they continued to overcharge for their products at Sukkot time, he would rule that even broken myrtles may be used for the four species and thus eliminate the demand.[9] As Pesah approached, when the merchants were overcharging for pots, he gave them another ultimatum:

---

[4] BT *Berakhot* 18b c. SA II:552.

[5] BT *Berakhot* 30a; *Bava Batra* 42b.

[6] See n. 4.

[7] BT *Bava Metzia* 85b–86a c. SA II:553.

[8] Ibid.

[9] BT *Sukkah* 34b.

either they lower their prices or he would permit people to keep their hametz pots on Pesah.[10] The merchants gave in.

Shmuel used his expertise not only in Torah matters but also in medicine.

> I know the cure for all but three things: eating bitter dates on an empty stomach, girding one's loins with a damp flaxen cord, and eating bread and not walking afterward.[11]

He was able to identify the cause of death in an animal carcass[12] and the age of a fetus.[13] Though he was known as the inventor of eye ointment, he praised hygiene as the greatest preventative. "A drop of cold water in the morning and bathing the hands and feet in hot water in the evening is better than all the eye ointments in the world."[14] He would cure people without their knowing that they were being treated. When Rabbi Yehuda ha-Nasi had an eye infection and refused medication, Shmuel placed some ointment on his pillow and he was cured overnight.[15] Rav had a more unpleasant experience when Shmuel applied his ingenuity to cure Rav's chronic stomach troubles.

> Shmuel took him into his house and fed him barley bread and fish pie with strong liquor, but did not show him where

---

[10] BT *Pesahim* 30a.

[11] BT *Bava Metzia* 113b.

[12] BT *Hullin* 59a c. SA II:531.

[13] BT *Niddah* 25a c. SA II:557.

[14] BT *Shabbat* 108b.

[15] See n. 7 above.

the bathroom was. Rav then cursed him for causing him pain.[16]

His knowledge was of the heavenly bodies[17] earned him the title "Shmuel the Moon Expert."[18] He claimed:

> I am as familiar with the paths of heaven as with the streets of Nehardea [his hometown], with the exception of the comet, about which I am ignorant.[19]

It is possible that he was not as knowledgeable as he claimed, as Abba the father of Rabbi Simlai rejected Shmuel's boast that he was capable of making a calendar predicting the new lunar months for all of the Diaspora.[20] Perhaps some gaps in his knowledge could be forgiven, as he studied astronomy only while he was in the bathroom.[21]

Irrespective of his confidence in his own abilities, Shmuel paid a great deal of respect to other well-known scholars, such as Rabbi Addah bar Ahavah,[22] Rav Assi,[23] and Mar Ukbah.[24] His closest relationship was with his colleague, Rav. He "showed deference to Rav"[25] and insisted that Rav sit

---

[16] BT *Shabbat* 108a c. SA II:524.

[17] BT *Hullin* 95b.

[18] Rashi *Bava Metzia* 65b s.v. "*Shmuel Yarchina'ah.*"

[19] BT *Berakhot* 58b c. SA II:554.

[20] BT *Rosh ha-Shannah* 20b.

[21] *Devarim Rabbah* 8:4 c. SA II:555.

[22] BT *Taanit* 20b c. SA II:534.

[23] BT *Bava Kama* 80b c. SA II:525.

[24] BT *Mo'ed Katan* 16b c. SA II:563.

[25] BT *Megillah* 24a.

ahead of him in the court of the *resh galuta*.[26] In turn, Rav insisted that Shmuel enter a room first.[27] Shmuel ruled that a *prozbul* can only be written by a bet din of stature, namely only Rav's or his own.[28] Although they disagreed on many points, whenever one visited the other's community, he would behave according to the views held by the host.[29]

When Rav passed away, Shmuel "tore thirteen garments and said, "The only man who intimidated me is gone."[30]

Yet although he deferred to the opinions of those whom he respected, he did not give in when he thought that his own views were superior. After the redaction of the Mishna, it was believed that scholars no longer had the authority to argue with tannaim whose views had already been placed into the canon.[31] However, Shmuel went against this trend in three places, expressing his opinion against the social norms.

In a discussion regarding the source for the permissibility of violating Shabbat in order to save a life, the Talmud cites two tannaitic opinions. Elsewhere, it cites four tannaitic opinions to prove that the book of Esther was "composed by means of the Holy Spirit." In the search for the biblical source for permission to renege on a vow, four tannaitic opinons are cited as well. In all these cases, Shmuel brazenly stated, "Had I been there, I would have given a proof superior to all."

What can the later scholars do with such statements? Shmuel broke the rules, putting his assurance in his ability above the weight carried by

---

[26] JT *Taanit* 4:2 c. SA II:533.

[27] See n. 23 above.

[28] BT *Gittin* 36b.

[29] BT *Eruvin* 94a.

[30] BT *Mo'ed Katan* 24a c. SA II:545.

[31] "[Amoraim were] not permitted to dispute a statement of the Mishnah or even of a *baraita*. If in the course of the discussion it emerged that his opinion conflicted with that of the Mishnah, his view was rejected" (Shmuel Safrai, "Amoraim," *Encyclopaedia Judaica*).

senior scholars. Ultimately, Shmuel's confidence in his teachings proved contagious; the later scholars agreed in all three cases that regardless of when he was born, Shmuel was correct, since

> All the proofs can be refuted except that of Shmuel, which cannot be refuted.... Against the proof of Shmuel certainly no decisive objection can be brought.[32]

From the time that Shmuel's father defended him from the abuses of an inept teacher, Shmuel began to develop the confidence he needed to speak his mind irrespective of the authority of that he challenged. It was this ability of Shmuel that was held up by the scholars as a living example of the popular saying "Better a single sharp pepper than a basket full of pumpkins," which they took to mean, "Better one sharp *amora* than a number of dull *tannaim.*"[33]

---

[32] See n. 1 above.

[33] Interpretation of the Arukh cited in Steinsaltz *Megillah* ad loc.

RAV ZEIRA

(c. 300 CE)

The very climate of the Land of Israel makes one wise.[1]

"THE LAND OF ISRAEL is like the World to Come," goes the cynical joke. "Every Jew wants to be there, but nobody wants to do what it takes to get there." Still, throughout Jewish history, there were some outstanding individuals whose passion for the land was so strong that they left the comfort of their birthplaces to "rise up" and go to Israel. Among the scholars, Rav Zeira was such an individual.

Rav Zeira had plenty of reasons to stay in his birthplace in Babylon. He was a well-respected scholar, heir to the traditions of the great Babylonian scholars Rav,[2] Shmuel,[3] Rav Huna, and his teacher, Yehuda ben Yehezkel.[4] He had students eager to learn from him.[5] His peers and teachers put a great deal of pressure on him to stay in the Diaspora, citing religious reasons for not making the move themselves.

At the head of this school of thought was Rav Zeira's own teacher, Rabbi Yehuda. "Living in Babylon has the same value as living in Israel," Rabbi Yehuda taught.[6] "It is forbidden to leave Babylon to go to any

---

[1] BT *Bava Batra* 158b.

[2] BT *Bekhorot* 39b.

[3] *Eikha Rabba* IV:23.

[4] BT *Taanit* 7a c. SA II:497.

[5] BT *Taanit* 7a c. SA II:497.

[6] BT *Ketubbot* 111a.

country."[7] Finally, since it was clear that God wanted his people to stay in Babylon and not to move to Israel until a divinely appointed time somewhere in the future, anyone who made *aliyah* transgressed a commandment in the Torah.[8]

Rav Zeira needed strong motivation that would enable him to withstand these pressures. That motivation came from his love of Israel. Although he was normally a stickler for tradition,[9] in this case he broke with his master and interpreted the law in his own fashion. It is not like Rabbi Yehuda claims, rather when the verse says "They will be carried to Babylon and be there until the day that I remember them," it refers only to the Temple vessels, not the people of Israel. Rabbi Yehuda's response is also incorrect, for the verse "I adjure you, daughters of Jerusalem… that ye awaken not, nor stir up love, until it please" only means "that all the people should not go up to Israel en masse." And thus the argument went on.[10]

Although Rav Zeira was not able to convince his teacher of the validity of his position, this did not stop him. Rav Zeira simply avoided him and made aliyah behind his back.[11]

Once he was on his way to Israel, nothing stood in his way. Upon reaching the Jordan, there were no boats available. One story is told that, unable to wait, he crossed a rope bridge into Israel.[12] Another version has him swimming fully clothed across the Jordan River.[13] If the bridge was as unsteady as the shouting onlookers warned him, perhaps both accounts are true. Either way, nothing was going to make him wait. He said, "If neither

---

[7] Ibid.

[8] BT *Ketubbot* 110b–111a.

[9] JT *Shabbat* 1:2 c. SA II:493, BT *Eruvin* 65a c. SA II:494.

[10] Ibid.

[11] BT *Shabbat* 41 c. SA II:500.

[12] BT *Ketubbot* 112a c. SA II:502.

[13] JT *Shavuot* 4:9 c. SA II:503.

Moshe nor Aharon was deemed worthy of entering this land, then who says that I will always be found worthy?"[14]

However, it was not only the Land of Israel that Rav Zeira yearned for. He wanted to be part of the culture. He did not wish to be merely a scholar from Babylon who had made *aliyah,* but rather a scholar of the Land of Israel. Even while he still lived in Babylon, whenever he heard that a scholar would be visiting Israel, he would send him with questions to confirm various Israeli traditions.[15] When he set out on his *aliyah,* he completed forty fasts (or one hundred!) to help him forget the Babylonian method of study that he had used for so many years so that he would fit in with the Israeli scholars. (One hopes that these fasts were more successful than the ones he undertook in order to make himself immune to the pain of fire. His experiments with sitting on a burning oven earned him the nickname "Scorched-thighs").[16] After all, he reasoned, what possible advantage could the scholars in Babylon have over the scholars in Israel? As Rav Zeira said: "The very climate of the Land of Israel makes one wise," and "Even the ordinary conversation of the people of the Land of Israel is Torah."[17]

His absorption was not easy. Despite the great efforts that he made to become a true Israeli, he still suffered discrimination due to his origins.

> When R. Zeira once went to the market to buy some goods, the shopkeeper said to him, "Get out of here, you Babylonian, whose ancestors destroyed the Temple!"

---

[14] See note 11 above.

[15] BT *Eruvin* 80a, BT *Bava Metzia* 43b.

[16] BT *Bava Metzia* 85a c. SA II:504. For the discrepancy between the number of fasts, see *Dikdukei Sofrim* ad loc. (248).

[17] *Vayikra Rabba* 34:7.

It was not until later that Rav Zeira understood that the shopkeeper was expressing a common view in Israel, one that Rav Zeira came to agree with: "Had the Israelites in Ezra's time made *aliyah* en masse from Babylon, the Second Temple would not have been destroyed."[18]

His alien status not only made him subject to insults, but also made him an open target of unsavory characters. A certain butcher who amused himself with the misfortunes of others once told Rav Zeira that in Israel, a piece of meat costs "fifty small coins and a stroke of the lash." At first Rav Zeira offered him more money in place of the lash, but in the end he capitulated, thinking that he must follow the customs of his new home. When later asked about the incident, he recalled, "I was not angry at all. I just thought that was the custom here."[19]

All his hardships paid off in the end. He was ordained, as only scholars in the land of Israel can be. He is quoted over one hundred thirty times in the Jerusalem Talmud, which was compiled in the Land of Israel.

And when he died, he was eulogized:

> The Land of Babylon conceived and bore him;
>
> the Land of Beauty made him great.
>
> Now Tiberias mourns,
>
> for she has lost her most precious jewel.[20]

In the end, the Land of Israel came to love him as much as he loved her.

---

[18] *Shir ha-Shirim Rabbah* 8:9.

[19] JT *Berakhot* 2:8 c. SA II:505.

[20] BT *Moed Katan* 25b c. SA II:515.

History in the Aggadic Narratives

The teachings of the scholars are not history books in which the authors record events that took place.
–Rabbi Yehuda Loew (Maharal of Prague), *Be'er Hagolah*, Chapter 6

ALTHOUGH THIS WORK contains descriptions of figures from the past, it is not a history book in the proper sense. This is true to the methodology and spirit of aggadic (non-halakhic) literature, which pays little attention to historical detail. The major events of their time, such as the factionalism and civil wars of the Second Temple era and the Bar Kokhba revolt, are only briefly mentioned a handful of times in the literature.[1] Other major occurrences, such as the attempt to build the Third Temple under Julian and the prevalent place of Zoroastrianism in Babylon, are not mentioned at all.[2]

---

[1] For references to Bar Kokbha, see Samuel Abramsky, "Bar Kokhba," *Encyclopaedia Judaica* (CD-ROM edition, Israel: 1997). The material on the factionalism and civil wars during the Second Temple era is so scant that even in Artscroll's Tisha be-Av primer, which claims to be based on "Talmudic and traditional sources" and cites aggadic narratives as history, the sections on this subject are based solely on Josephus (Avrohom Chaim Feuer and Shimon Finkelman, *Tishah B'Av: Texts, Readings, and Insights* [1992], 128–132.

[2] For a listing of sources that attempt to find references to the building of the Temple under Julian, see David Levenson, "The Ancient and Medieval Sources for the Emperor Julian's Attempt to Rebuild the Jerusalem Temple." *Journal for the Study of Judaism* 35 (4): 409–410 n. 1). The scholarly consensus agrees with Levenson that "The first Jewish reports of the incident do not appear until the sixteenth century" (409).

Though Yaakov Elman in "Acculturation to Elite Persian Norms and Modes of Thought in the Babylonian Jewish Community of Late Antiquity" (*Neti'ot le-David: Jubilee Volume for David Weiss Halivni*, edited by Yaakov Elman, Ephraim

Clearly, the purpose of aggadic literature is theological and moral rather than historical. This is not to say that Hazal did not value the study of history. Rather, they did not wish to limit the application of their literature to something so temporal as their own biographies and local politics.

For example, the Talmud (BT *Yevamot* 62b) tells of the tragic deaths of the students of Rabbi Akiva. The scholarly consensus is that Rabbi Akiva's students were killed during the Bar Kokhba uprising.[3] However, the Talmud makes no mention of this, saying only that "they all died at the same time because they did not respect one another." Hazal sought to give a reason for their deaths that is above history. Lack of respect for our fellow human being is a problem that has been present in every generation, and in the long term it is more meaningful than a particular military encounter. Hazal are concerned with the eternal rather than the temporal, the moral rather than the historical.

That said, the long-standing scholarly debate regarding the historical accuracy of the tales and the attribution of quotes to specific scholars[4] has little bearing on the intrinsic meaning of the text. In a slightly different context, Rambam argues strongly that one should concern oneself with the moral-theological meaning of aggadah rather than the literal one.[5] In our day,

---

Bezalel Halivni and Zvi Arie Steinfeld, 31–56 [2004]) convincingly demonstrates that "Middle Persian attitudes and doctrines made inroads in many areas of Babylonian rabbinic elite culture, in law, in theology, and in general cultural attitudes" (56), there is still no mention of any Zoroastrian ideas or figures as Zoroastrian per se in the Talmud. The closest the Talmud comes to mentioning this issue is Shmuel's discussion with King Shapur in which he mentions the king's rivalry with Rome (BT *Berakhot* 56a, *Moed Katan* 26a).

[3] See comments in the Steinsaltz edition of *Yevamot* (Israel Institute for Talmudic Publications), 264, *Iyunim*, s.v. *"shnem assar elef zugim."*

[4] For a survey of opinions see Richard Lee Kalmin, *Sages, Stories, Authors, and Editors in Rabbinic Babylonia* (Brown University, 1994) 2–3 (nn. 3–6).

[5] Rambam, *Commentary on the Mishna*: Sanhedrin, Chapter 10. For an explication of Rambam's position, see Simi Peters, *Learning to Read Midrash*, Urim, 103–104.

one could emphasize this point regarding the choice of the theological meaning over the historical one, the literary over the literal. For example, the primary biographical sources that are quoted about Rabbi Akiva span about one thousand years, from the Mishna to Rashi.[6] A responsible historian would be rightfully skeptical about the accuracy of these tales. Why would Rashi, writing in the eleventh century, be the first person to put into writing a tradition about Rabbi Akiva that would be one thousand years old if it were accurate? But this question is irrelevant to the purpose of learning Torah.[7] The importance of a tradition lies not in its historical accuracy but rather in its moral meaning. The scholars who transmitted (or invented) this tradition did not intend to convey biographical information about the Rabbi Akiva who lived in Palestine during the first two centuries of the Common Era, but rather about Rabbi Akiva the literary figure, who is a central character in the drama of the Jewish people.[8] To support this claim, one only

---

[6] See chapter on Rabbi Akiva above, n. 27.

[7] "Our first task is therefore to read it in a way that respects its givens and its conventions, without mixing in the questions arising for a philologist or a historian to the meaning that derives from its juxtapositions. Did audiences in Shakespeare's theatre spend their time showing off their critical sense by pointing out that there were only wooden boards where the stage sign indicated a place of a forest?" Emmanuel Levinas, *Nine Talmudic Readings* (translated by Annette Arnowicz, Indiana University Press, 1990), 5.

[8] "[The scholars] might choose as protagonists early rabbis who possessed or were said to possess some outstanding characteristic which particularly suited the author's message. The blindness of Rav Sheshet, a prominent Talmudic rabbi, might make him an especially fitting subject of a story which teaches that spiritual insight is far more powerful than physical sight. Even long after his death, [Rav] Sheshet might be made the protagonist of such a tale, for perhaps he had come to be the archetypical blind scholar, whose immense spiritual gifts more than compensated for his physical shortcomings" (Kalmin 7).

"R.[abbi Shimshon Raphael] Hirsch writes, 'It is possible that some of [the stories in the Talmud and Midrash] were stated only in the manner of rhetorical invention [Heb. *hamza'at meliza*], for some ethical or educational goal...'. (quoted by Mordekhai Breuer, *'Ma'amar ha-Rav S.R. Hirsch z.z.l al Aggadot Hazal,' Ha-*

has to see the dearth of biographical information about any member of Hazal in order to learn how little the aggadah is concerned with transmitting history. As one scholar puts it, "…Not one of these 3,820 men is it possible to write a biography in the serious sense of the word. Strictly speaking, little biographical information is furnished. Very often attributions are contradictory and uncertain.…"[9]

The same message applies regarding the miraculous events described in the aggadah. Soon after the completion of the Talmud, scholars already debated whether or not the miracles that are found within its pages had actually occurred.[10] However, from our perspective (which I believe is the perspective of the talmudic scholars themselves), this argument is hardly relevant. Once we establish that the primary meaning of the text is not historical but rather moral, then the issue of whether the miracles actually occurred or not takes on secondary importance at most. In the words of Rabbi Shlomo Yosef Zevin,

> The miraculous, wonderful, and supernatural tales that are found in the two Talmuds about the scholars… are not told as ends in themselves, such as a miracle for the sake of the miracle and a wonder for the sake of a wonder. Rather the goal is to conclude with "therefore" and to teach a lesson

Ma'ayan, 16, No.2 [*Tevet* 5736], 14." c. Chaim Eisen, "Maharal's *Be'er ha-Golah* and His Revolution in Aggadic Scholarship," *Hakira* 4 [Winter 2007], n.79.

[9] Judah Goldin, "Toward a Profile of the Tanna, Aqiba ben Joseph." *Studies in Midrash and Related Literature* (edited by Barry L. Eichler and Jeffrey H. Tigay; 1988), 299.

[10] See the approaches of Rav Shmuel ben Hofni Gaon and Rav Hai Gaon relating to the "four went into the orchard" narrative quoted in *Otzar ha-Geonim: Hagigah* (edited by B. Lewin; Hebrew University Publishing), 13, and the debate between Rav Nutrani Gaon and Rabbeinu Hananel on the miracles in the oven of Akhnai story quoted in Steinsaltz edition of *Bava Metzia* (Israel Institute for Talmudic Publications) 248, *Iyunim* s.v. "*haruv, emat hamayim.*" For Rambam's approach, see n. 5 above.

that is religiously educational or the like. Pay attention and you'll see.[11]

---

[11] Shlomo Yosef Zevin, *Sipurei Hassidim – Torah* (2002), 12.

Glossary of Hebrew Terms

Adam ha-Rishon – Adam (the first man)

aggadah – narrative portions of the Talmud (see *Talmud*)

Aharon – Aaron (Moses's brother, the first High Priest)

aliyah – to move to the Land of Israel (literally: "ascend")

amora'im (s. *amora*) – scholars who lived between the completion of the Mishna (see *Mishna*) and completion of the Talmud (see *Talmud*) (about 200–500 CE)

Bavli – the Babylonian Talmud (see *Talmud*), which is of primary importance in Jewish law and tradition

Bet ha-Mikdash – Jewish Temple that stood in Jerusalem

Bet Hillel – disciples of Hillel the Elder (literally "House of Hillel")

berakhot – blessings

Binyamin – tribe of Benjamin

birkat ha-mazon – grace after meals

brit milah – circumcision ceremony (referred to in Eastern European pronunciation as "bris")

Eliyahu ha-Navi – Elijah the Prophet, who in aggadic literature occasionally visits individuals in order to help them.

erev Shabbat – Friday before Shabbat (see Shabbat)

halakha (pl. *halakhot*, adj. halakhic) – Jewish law

hametz – leavening or leavened products, such as bread, that are prohibited on Passover

Hanukkah – eight-day festival that takes place in the winter

havdala – ceremony that takes place at the end of the Sabbath

Hazal – the scholars found in the Mishna (see *Mishna*), Talmud (see *Talmud*), and Midrash. (Literally an acronym for "Our scholars, may they be remembered for good")

huppah – wedding canopy

Ketuvim – Writings (third section of the Bible)

Kohen – a member of the priestly class descended from Aharon

Kohen Gadol – High Priest

ma'aser – tithe that is taken from produce

midrash (pl. *midrashim*) – genre of rabbinic literature usually consisting of expositions on the Bible

Mishna – Collection of laws and traditions edited by Rabbi Yehuda ha-Nasi

mitzvot – commandments, good deeds

Moshe, Moshe Rabbeinu – Moses

Nasi – title of Head of the High Court (Sanhedrin) (literally "prince")

Nevi'im – Prophets (second section of Bible)

Pesah – Passover, eight-day festival that takes place in the spring

prozbul – legal document that allows a creditor to collect his due after the sabbatical year in light of the prohibition against this

resh galuta – lay head of the Babylonian Jewish community, referred to in English as the Exilarch

Rosh ha-Shannah – festival of New Year that takes place in the fall

Rosh Hodesh – festival of the New (lunar) Month

Sanhedrin – High Court of Jewish Law

Seder – ceremonial meal held on the first night of Passover

Shabbat – Jewish Sabbath, that takes place from sunset Friday to nightfall Saturday

Shabbat candles – candles that are lit immediately before the Sabbath begins

Shema – prayer that begins with the verse "Hear, O Israel" (Deuteronomy 6:4)

shemittah – sabbatical year

Shir ha-Shirim – The Song of Songs (book in the Bible)

Sifra – compilations of primarily legal discussions on the book of Leviticus

Sifre – compilations of primarily legal discussions on the books of Numbers and Deuteronomy

Sukkah – booth that is lived in during the Sukkot festival in the fall

Talmud (adj. Talmudic) – compliations (see *Bavli, Yerushalmi*) of discussions on Jewish laws and traditions, loosely based on the Mishna (see Mishna)

Tanakh – The Bible (Old Testament)

Tannaim (adj. Tannaitic) – scholars whose views are recorded in the Mishna (see Mishna)

tekhelet – a type of indigo or azure dye

tefillah – prayer

Torah – Literally, the books of Genesis, Exodus, Leviticus, Numbers, and Deuteronomy, but is also used in reference to all Jewish learning and texts.

Tosefta – a compilation of laws and traditions edited around the same time as the Mishna (see *Mishna*), though not given the same legal importance

tzara'at – a type of infection that appears on skin, clothing, and buildings

Va-yikra – The Book of Leviticus (the third book of the Pentateuch)

Yehuda – the tribe of Judah

Yerushalmi – The Palestinian (or Jerusalem) Talmud (see *Talmud*), which was completed in the Land of Israel

Yom Kippur – The Day of Atonement

About the Author

Jonathan Duker received his rabbinical ordination from the Chief Rabbinate of Israel and from Yeshivat Chovevei Torah. He earned his B.A. and M.A. in Jewish history from Yeshiva University. Rabbi Duker has been teaching rabbinic thought and halakha in Israel since his aliyah in the summer of 2004. He lives in Beit Shemesh with his wife Susan and their children.